Writing Romance in the 21st Century: Plotting and Planning

Non-Fiction

Vanessa Grant

Published by Muse Creations Inc, 2019.

Table of Contents

Praise for Previous Editions 1
Author's Note 2
1: A Successful Romance Novel 4
2. Controversial Issues in Romance Novels 16
3: Powerful Archetypes for your Characters 22
4: Getting Ideas: the Story Spark 30
6: Character Driven Plotting: | Growing a Couple 50
7: More About Characters 63
8: Conflict & Struggle 72
9: Territory, the Bridge Between Character & Conflict 85
10: The Power of Setting 97
11: Scene & Sequel — the Skin and Bones of Story 107
12: The Hero's Journey — | the Heart and Soul of Story 118
13: Diversity and Inclusivity 128
14: A Personal Note about Diversity | from Vanessa Grant 142
Copyright 143

This book is dedicated to all those wonderful readers and storytellers who contributed their wisdom, feedback, and experience to this book

...and to Brian, my friend, lover, partner, and co-adventurer for over 40 years With love, always.

Praise for Previous Editions ...

"Essential for all aspiring romance writers."
— Jo Beverley, NYT Bestselling Author

"It is by far the best writing book I've ever read. Five stars for Vanessa."
— The Writer's Markets Report, National Writer's Monthly

"*Writing Romance* is a kind of how-to-do-it-yourself romance writer's workshop under one cover, and will reward the serious reader by [offering] helpful, practical advice so necessary to successfully break into print in the romance field. Highly recommended!"
— Midlist Book Review

"*Writing Romance* is a thoroughly professional guide to a business that generates close to $1 billion a year."
— Canadian Book Review Annual

Author's Note

"The day the power of love overrules the love of power, the world will know peace." — *Mahatma Gandhi*

THE 21st Century is an exciting time for authors. There are more books being published than ever before. The romance genre has expanded, and a variety of strong, romantic sub-genres have appeared, including young adult, sweet traditional, contemporary, sexy, erotic, urban fantasy, futuristic, and LGBTQ+. Storytellers and writers are writing about a broader, more diverse world.

Despite these changes, the heart of romance remains unchanged. Romantic love features in almost all our fiction, and in ballads, poetry, movies, and dreams. Half of all paperbacks sold are romance novels, stories in which two people struggle to overcome the obstacles to their romantic love. The need to love and be loved is embedded deep in our DNA and our brains. We are stronger together when we love and are loved, forging bonds for a lifetime. Because love matters, we dream about love, fantasize about love, and tell stories about love.

Whatever subgenre of romance you want to write, and whether romance is the primary focus of your story, or a sub-plot for your mystery, science fiction, fantasy, historical or futuristic novel, the 21st century is calling for you to write about love realistically.

Read romances. Ask yourself what makes each one exciting, romantic, or fulfilling. Watch how people behave when they are in love. Look for the problems that make happy-ever-after difficult for lovers

WRITING ROMANCE IN THE 21ST CENTURY: PLOTTING AND PLANNING

and explore how these problems can be overcome. Read this book, then start planning, plotting, and writing your own romance—and don't forget to have fun while you're doing it!

1: A Successful Romance Novel

"We live our lives within a single viewpoint. We never get out of it — never really live in another person's head and heart. So if we are to make our fiction as lifelike as possible, shouldn't we present the story from a single viewpoint, too, letting the reader experience the story just as [they experience] real life?" — Jack M. Bickham, *Writing and Selling your Novel*

A SINGLE VIEWPOINT

THE READER WHO OPENS a romance novel is looking for someone to identify with, someone with whom they can share a journey of love. The fictional characters you create to star in your novel's leading role will be the lovers through whose eyes, ears, mind and heart your readers experience the story.

If you're having a challenge deciding which of your lovers to choose as the primary protagonist, I recommend following the advice given by Jack Bickham in his book, *Writing and Selling Your Novel*.

PICK THE PERSON ...

- who will be at the center of the action;
- who will have everything to risk;
- whose struggle toward a goal is the fuel driving the story;
- and who will be moved — changed — by the outcome.

WRITING ROMANCE IN THE 21ST CENTURY: PLOTTING AND PLANNING

Whether your chosen character is male, female, transgender, non-gendered, human, Martian, werewolf, vampire, or shapeshifter: this is your protagonist, your hero.

This is the person through whose eyes your reader will experience the story.

THE STORY QUESTION

A GOOD NOVEL BEGINS by stirring a question in the reader's mind. A romance novel's story question is usually something along the lines of ...

- Can my protagonist overcome these problems and find true love and partnership?
- Can love triumph over loss and adversity?

This story question must remain the focus throughout the story and should never be fully answered until the end of the novel.

AN EMPOWERING THEME

THE BEST LOVE STORIES are fantasies in which the deep emotional values of love, family, partnership and loyalty eventually emerge victorious over lesser values.

Although most romances have a positive ending, the power of love can triumph even when the ending has elements of loss.

James Cameron and Ed Marsh's powerful story *Titanic* opens with Rose as an elderly woman surrounded by photographs showing the full, adventurous life she has led. The wreckage of *Titanic* has been discovered, and with it, an artist's pencil drawing of a naked young woman.

The woman is Rose, and the story has shifted back in time to April 10, 1912. Rose is a young woman boarding the doomed *Titanic* with her mother. Accompanying them is Rose's wealthy fiancé, chosen by her mother to secure the family's finances.

Rose's visible sadness is a stark contrast to the joyful life force of Jack, a penniless artist who wins his below-decks passage on *Titanic*'s maiden voyage in a poker game.

Later, when Rose climbs over the rails in a desperate attempt to escape her life, Jack rescues her, creating a bond between them. While the *Titanic* sails toward disaster, Jack ignores the barriers between upper and lower class, showing Rose a below-decks world free of upper-class restrictions.

When Rose and Jack fall in love, her fiancé intervenes, framing Jack for a crime he didn't commit, and arranging to have him locked up below-decks. While *Titanic* sinks, Rose heroically fights to free Jack from handcuffs below-decks and the couple run to escape the doomed ship.

Too late for the lifeboats, they jump off the sinking ship into the ocean.

Clinging to a piece of floating wreckage that can support only one of them, Jack's life-force drains into the freezing water. Before he dies, he urges Rose to fight for her life and her dreams.

Although Rose has lost the man she loves, she grasps at life when she hears rescuers in the distance, blowing the whistle hanging from her life vest. Later, shivering under a blanket sitting on the deck of the rescue boat, she sees her fiancé searching for her. Keeping her promise to Jack, Rose choses a life of freedom and turns her back on her wealthy fiancé.

Rose is no longer powerless, ruled by others, and she's not alone. Jack will always be in her heart. The entire movie is an affirmation of the power of love over loss and adversity.

WRITING ROMANCE IN THE 21ST CENTURY: PLOTTING AND PLANNING

DESIGNING FICTIONAL LOVERS

"People who are more isolated than they want to be are less happy, their health declines earlier in midlife, their brain function declines sooner, and they live shorter lives than people who are not lonely," — Dr. Robert Waldinger, Director, Harvard Study of Adult Development.

HUMANS ARE PACK ANIMALS, incomplete living in isolation. As a creator, your job is to ...

- to design lovers who complete each other's missing parts;
- to give each lover the strength and commitment to overcome the life obstacles you plan to put in their way;
- and to guide your lovers' individual journeys through loss, adversity, joy and love until they forge a resilient and loving lifelong partnership.

If you can do all this for your lovers, they'll be happier. They'll be smarter. They'll live longer.

Your reader wants to identify with your lovers, to care about them, to suffer with them, and most of all — to believe in them. Your lovers need not be overwhelmingly handsome, beautiful, powerful or successful, so long as they come alive for both you and your reader.

OVERCOMING OBSTACLES

"Fiction is just one damned thing after another. If your hero, however likable he may be, confronts his problem, however desperate it may be, and just plain goes ahead and solves it, you have not got something Publishers Weekly is going to call 'a real page turner.' But if he keeps

dodging one menace only to rush headlong into the jaws of another, and if his prospects keep getting worse, and if he winds up with more perils than Pauline, then you just might be on the right track." — Lawrence Block, *Telling Lies for Fun & Profit*

IF YOU'RE GOING TO create an interesting story, you'll need to put obstacles in the way of your lovers' happy ending, challenges they strive to overcome while your readers keep turning pages, staying up late to finish the book.

- In *Titanic*, Rose and Jack fight overwhelming external obstacles to their love. Rose's mother and her abusive fiancé are both determined to do anything it takes to get rid of Jack. The rigid class system of the early 20th century fully supports those efforts.

- As with *Titanic,* in many great romances the lovers must triumph over their own limitations and personal scars. This has been true of romantic storytelling over the decades.

- Erich Segal's *Love Story* was originally written as a screenplay but was adapted as a novel, and released ten months before the December 1970 movie as a preview of sorts. This achingly beautiful romance became the top selling North American novel of 1970 and was translated into 20 languages. I still remember the opening paragraph of this beautiful love story which I read in the early 1970s …

"What can you say about a twenty-five-year-old-girl who died? That she was beautiful. And brilliant. That she loved Mozart and Bach. And the Beatles. And me." — Erich Segal, *Love Story*

WRITING ROMANCE IN THE 21ST CENTURY: PLOTTING AND PLANNING

- Bobby Hutchinson's *Draw Down the Moon* (1987) is the story of how a woman bound by a wheelchair heals the heart of an emotionally scarred hostage negotiator.
- In the beautiful movie *Forest Gump* (1994), Tom Hanks played a mentally slow and physically challenged man. Gump finally finds happiness with his longtime school friend Jenny and their young son shortly before Jenny dies.
- Mary Balogh's historical novel *Silent Melody* (1997) tells the story of a deaf woman's fight to win the heart of the man she loves.
- In Meredith Russo's multiple award-winning novel, *If I was Your Girl* (2016), teenage Amanda wants nothing more than to make friends and fit into her new high school. But when she meets and falls in love with fellow student Grant, she's terrified that telling him she used to be a boy will cost her both her new life, and her new love.

Just like you and I, our fictional lovers must have fears, dreams, hopes, a personal history, and emotional baggage. Whether tragically disabled or physically, mentally, and emotionally healthy, your lovers need strong personality characteristics and at least one believable and non-trivial weakness or flaw which you will help them to overcome.

INITIAL CONFLICT

MOST GOOD STORIES BEGIN with the viewpoint character facing an initial problem or situation which engages the reader. By the time the immediate problem is solved, other problems have developed to engage the reader. This initial conflict should reveal enough about the viewpoint character and/or the story to stir the reader's interest and curiosity.

AN EMOTIONALLY INTENSE CORE CONFLICT

AS YOUR FICTIONAL LOVERS come to know each other, new obstacles to their happy ending appear. In the strongest stories, conflict grows out of the characteristics, goals, and life challenges of the lovers, revealing a core difficulty between them which must be resolved before they can have a successful relationship.

APPROPRIATE SENSUALITY

IN A SUCCESSFUL ROMANCE novel, the degree of sexual intimacy on the page should be appropriate to the characters, the story, the genre, and consistent with the author's own comfort level.

In the traditional and inspirational romance novels written before the 1970s, love scenes were rarely described explicitly. Now, four decades later, the romance market includes a variety of romance sub-genres, each with its own expectations about how sexual intimacy is handled. Pick the level of sexuality and sensuality that you feel most comfortable reading, and writing!

The following is the listing of romance sub-genres I've seen online: Anthologies, Contemporary, Erotica, Fantasy, Gothic, Historical, Holidays, Inspirational, LGBT, Medieval Historical, Military, Multicultural & Interracial, Mystery & Suspense, New Adult, Paranormal, Romantic Comedy, Science Fiction, Scottish Historical Romance, Sports, Time Travel, Western.

Readers in each of these romance sub-genres have a general expectation about the kind of story they'll get when they purchase the book. For example:

- *Contemporary Romance* readers expect a romantic story involving both emotional and physical intimacy. Any sex

WRITING ROMANCE IN THE 21ST CENTURY: PLOTTING AND PLANNING

scenes will probably be described with a strong focus on the viewpoint character's emotional response.

- *Erotica Romance* readers expect a sexy romance in which the sexual encounters are more frequent and more graphically described than in contemporary romance.
- *Inspirational Romance* readers expect a deep emotional love story with a strong spiritual focus. If the characters do have sex during the story, it's unlikely to be described on the page, or if it is described, the description is likely to be romantic, not physically graphic.

Whatever the sub-genre, I believe the most powerful love scenes in romance are those in which the writer focuses on the emotions of the characters, not the clinical details of lovemaking.

AN INTRIGUING PLOT

TO HOLD THE READER'S interest, the events in your romance novel must be important to your characters. In a successful romance novel, the story or plot develops logically and naturally from character and conflict, and inevitably follows classic patterns of storytelling described in the following books, which I highly recommend for all storytellers.

RESOURCES:
WRITING FUNDAMENTALS AND TECHNIQUES

"I'll tell you right now that every aspiring writer should read The Elements of Style. Rule 17 in the chapter titled Principles of Composition is 'Omit needless words.' I will try to do that here." –Stephen King

WILLIAM STRUNK JR & E.B. WHITE: *The Elements of Style*. This little book is a wonderful guide for anyone who wants to develop clear, effective, and powerful writing. It's short; it's concise, it's useful, and it's still going strong after a century.

Strunk and White's *The Elements of Style* was chosen as one of *Time Magazine's* all-time top 100 nonfiction books, reporting that ...

"Strunk and White waded through the totality of our vast and complicated language and boiled it down to a terse 105 pages, including a glossary and index. No exhaustive explanations or sentence diagrams here — just 22 style rules and principles of composition, followed by "a few matters of form," a conclusive list of misused words and phrases and an all-encompassing "guide to style," composed ... by White. The Elements of Style is a timeless reminder of the simplicity of proper writing and is likely to remain a useful tool for years to come." — Erin Skarda, Time Magazine.

JACK M. BICKHAM: *Scene and Structure* (1999) and *Writing and Selling Your Novel* (1996). These books describe the structure of fiction, giving essential writing fundamentals and techniques with numerous examples of their use.

Bickham's *38 Most Common Fiction Writing Mistakes (and how to avoid them)*, is also well worth adding to your writing library. From Number 1. *Don't make excuses,* to Number 38. *Don't just sit there*, this book is filled with practical, no-nonsense advice for storytellers.

DWIGHT V. SWAIN's *Techniques of the Selling Writer (1965)*. Although Swain's writing tends to be *denser* than Bickham's more reader-friendly *Writing and Selling your Novel*. there's quite a bit of overlap in these books, but much that is unique in each. I recommend both these books for your writer's library. Note: Swain was Bickham's writing teacher, and Bickham's books are excellent at going beyond the instructions and giving practical examples of the techniques.

WRITING ROMANCE IN THE 21ST CENTURY: PLOTTING AND PLANNING

RESEARCHING YOUR STORY

WHEN YOU'RE WRITING about social issues and human psychological baggage, be sure to research the issue thoroughly. Check out fiction and non-fiction books dealing with the issue. Find someone, somewhere, who has faced this issue in a way that's consistent with your vision for your story and the characters you are creating. Prowl through the Internet, looking for authentic people, experts with credentials, check out Ted Talks on YouTube to identify experts in the field, and get a *feel* for positive ways to deal with that issue. Don't stop at the borders of your own experience.

When I was planning my women's fiction novel *Lifelines: Kate's Story*, I wanted to put my protagonist, Kate, in an ethical nightmare and I needed to be sure that her reactions were realistic.

Although I volunteered as a peer counsellor for a social service agency at the time and had taken several psychology and counselling courses, I needed a professional's feedback. I approached Marlene, my mentor at the agency where I volunteered, and she agreed to let me interview her. When we met, I asked her to do a role play, putting herself into the situation of my character, Kate, while I fed Marlene, step-by-step, the events leading to Kate's realization of the ethical mess she'd stumbled into.

In her role as Kate, Marlene gave me a running commentary on how she, as a counsellor and as a woman, would be thinking, feeling, and reacting. She was really getting into her role, and when we came to the moment when my character realizes the mess she's in, Marlene's reaction was exactly the kind of *Oh, Shit!* black moment that I hoped for.

With Marlene's help, I gained confidence in my story scenario and was able to move on with my book, knowing I was on the right track.

YOUR OWN ROMANCE NOVEL

Because each area of the romance genre has its own unique flavor, there's probably a place for your story somewhere in there. For the best chance of success, study market information before writing and submitting or self-publishing your story. If you are planning to self-publish your story, I recommend that you:

- have your book edited by a professional editor with experience in the romance genre, and
- seek out a group of other authors who are pursuing the self-publication route and are willing to share their experiences

SUMMARY: INGREDIENTS OF A SUCCESSFUL ROMANCE

A SUCCESSFUL ROMANCE ...

- Opens with a story question that stirs the reader's mind;
- Is empowering, affirming the values of love, family, and relationship;
- Has a sympathetic protagonist the reader can care about, and a love partner both the protagonist and the reader can fall in love with. These people are designed by you and made for each other!
- Begins with an interesting initial conflict or problem;
- Develops an emotionally intense core conflict;
- Keeps the heroic protagonist, love partner, and reader involved in continuing complications and problems for the characters (your plot);
- Is well researched;
- Has a level of sensuality appropriate to the characters and the story;
- Develops a black moment when all seems lost, and ...

WRITING ROMANCE IN THE 21ST CENTURY: PLOTTING AND PLANNING

- Concludes with an ending that satisfies the reader, affirming the values of love and positive relationships.

2. Controversial Issues in Romance Novels

FIFTY YEARS AGO, ROMANCE publishers would seldom buy a novel that dealt with controversial personal issues in a realistic way. Today, the extent to which a romance editor will be friendly toward a book dealing with a sensitive issue depends on the editor's personal taste, the market the publisher is interested in targeting, and the publisher's recent experiences with similar issues in the marketplace.

Here are only a few of the groundbreaking issues that have been tackled by romance authors over the last few decades:

- *Daphne Clair* — In *Marriage Under Fire (1983)* The protagonist, re-examining her life and her marriage, committed adultery against her husband. In *No Escape (1987)*, Clair's female protagonist abandoned the daughter she loved because she was terrified she might physically abuse her child. These are both very moving books.
- *Mary Kirk* — In *Phoenix Rising (1989)*, Mary Kirk's protagonist kidnapped her son from his abusive father and went on the run to protect him. In *Miracles (1990)*, Kirk's female hero falls in love with a man who has recovered from a near-death experience only to discover he's now a psychic healer. In *Embers (1991)*, her protagonist returns to the childhood home where she was an incest victim.
- *Judith Duncan* — In *Streets of Fire (1990)*, Duncan wrote a powerful romance in which an ex-prostitute and an injured ex-policeman struggled to find their happy ending.
- *Laurey Bright* — *An Interrupted Marriage (1994)*, tells the

WRITING ROMANCE IN THE 21ST CENTURY: PLOTTING AND PLANNING

story of a female hero who has spent two years in a mental hospital.

- *Mary Jo Putney* — In *One Perfect Rose (1997)*, Putney tackled the issue of death and dying; in *The Burning Point (2000)*, she explored the issue of physical abuse in marriage with sensitivity and hope; and in *The Spiral Path (2002)*, she explored survival of childhood abuse — all during a period when such issues were rarely seen in ro*mances*.
- *Meredith Russo* — *If I Was Your Girl (2016)* tells the turbulent, painful, and triumphant story of a transgender high school student finding both love and her place in the world.
- *Nora Roberts* — *Under Currents (2019)* is a romantic suspense novel that takes a deep dive into a horrific case of spousal and childhood abuse and the healing power of friendship, love, and enduring relationships over adversity.

"Roberts's latest is full of powerful, magnetic characters who have overcome terrible situations. Suspense and sensual romance are expertly combined in this riveting story."

— Publisher's Weekly

- J D Robb is a pseudonym used by Nora Roberts for her futuristic series of romantic crime novels. — #1 *Naked in Death* (1995) to #50 *Golden in Death* (2020). The series traces "murder cop" Eve Dallas's fight to bring justice to victims of violent crime, while struggling to live with traumatic childhood memories of violent physical and sexual abuse. What I admire most about this series is the skill with which Rob weaves the mystery elements into the evolving relationship between Eve and her love partner Roarke, both of whom are haunted by memories of abuse. The author deals with violence, controversial issues, and Eve's evolving ability to form and nurture positive relationships with others, making each book in the series a testament to the power of love to overcome loss and adversity.

Every era has its cluster of complex issues. As I revise this passage for 2019, the #MeToo movement has pushed the issue of sexual abuse to the forefront; the LGBTQ+ community's struggle for inclusivity has taken gender and sexual identity out of the closet and is receiving growing support.

WRITING ROMANCE IN THE 21ST CENTURY: PLOTTING AND PLANNING

Daphne Clair talks about...
CONTROVERSIAL ISSUES IN ROMANCE

SERIOUS MATTERS ARE dealt with successfully in romance by being individualized, given a personal face. One woman's efforts to overcome the effects of rape on her love life, or one man's battle with alcoholism for the sake of his relationship with a woman, described by a skilled and sincere writer, can illuminate, educate, comfort and influence, even mobilize. A reader who cares about your characters will gain understanding of their problems in a wider sense. Stories influence readers.

"Big" issues like saving whales or rain forests tend to overwhelm the story. If the heroine has reared a pet whale from birth, or lives in the threatened rain forest, there's a germ of a story — not about whales or rain forests but about two people. Does the sheltered but imprisoned whale represent the heroine's own need for security? Or does the hero's determination to build a road and hospital in the wild arise from guilt at failing to save his son from some tropical disease? And how does that affect the love story?

The issue should be central, not an extra that could be removed without affecting the romance. But a romance is not about a problem. It is about a person with a specific problem who falls in love with someone who at first compounds the problem and ultimately helps resolve it. The relationship between two people falling in love is at the heart of every romance.

DAPHNE CLAIR has written over 75 romantic novels written as Daphne Clair and Laurey Bright, with millions of readers worldwide, and a fat historical novel that was well-reviewed in her native New Zealand. She lives and works in the "winterless north" of New Zealand with her Netherlands-born husband, where they run a retreat for working writers; and with Robyn Donald, Daphne conducts romance writing workshops for aspiring writers.

Mary Jo Putney on...
CONTROVERSIAL ISSUES IN ROMANCE

TOO OFTEN POPULAR ENTERTAINMENT goes for the simple black and white story. Too often, the domestic violence story is the innocent wife and the evil husband who becomes a homicidal monster. That is a true story, played out all too often in the newspapers. But it is not the only story. Life is shades of gray and most humans have at least some violence in them, even if circumstances never cause it to manifest.

The characters in my novel *The Burning Point* married in passion and separated in violence. Can two such people ever get beyond the past to build a future based on love and maturity?

Sometimes. Such things do happen in real life. Donovan's youth, abusive childhood, and desperate emotional needs made him prone to emotional desperation and poor impulse control. Losing what he loved most pushed him into facing his flaws and overcoming them. Ironically, when he and Kate come together again, he is wiser and more in touch with himself. Kate had shifted everything under the carpet, a good short-term coping strategy, but one that left her emotionally diminished. Only by facing her own demons can she fully give and receive love.

Impossible in real life? Not at all. Romance is about hope and second chances, and that story is as valid as dark despair. In fact, I think that romance is a terrific place to explore difficult issues because of the safety net of a happy ending. Readers who never heard of Elisabeth Kubler-Ross can read about death and dying issues in my book *One*

WRITING ROMANCE IN THE 21ST CENTURY: PLOTTING AND PLANNING

Perfect Rose, knowing that the ending will be satisfying. Or read about childhood abuse in *The Spiral Path*. It's important to write about survivors as well as victims, and where better than in romance?

MARY JO PUTNEY *is a New York Times bestselling author who writes romances notable for intensity and psychological depth. Her most recent book is "Once a Scoundrel". She says the best part of being a writer is never having to wear pantyhose.*

3: Powerful Archetypes for your Characters

Myth is the secret opening through which the inexhaustible energies of the cosmos pour into human cultural manifestation.... — Joseph Campbell

THROUGHOUT TIME, POWERFUL character archetypes appear again and again in human myths and stories. In his 1949 publication of *The Hero with a Thousand Faces,* mythologist Joseph Campbell described these archetypes and the mythical and psychological functions they fill. More recently, Hollywood story consultant Christopher Vogler showed how these archetypes translate into modern fiction in his book, *The Writer's Journey: Mythic Structure for Writers*, which is now in its third edition.

To identify archetypes that fit your characters, think about the themes and characters you like reading about. Explore the different archetypes in this book and others, and experiment with them as building blocks for your own characters.

Although several of the archetypes that follow are specifically portrayed in mythology as male or female, the spirit of these archetypes can inhabit any character.

- *Wild Woman* - She's passionately and completely herself. She's certain of her identity, of who and what she is. She never needs to wear a mask or pretend to be someone she is not. This archetype is best described by the following quote in Clarissa Pinkola Estes book, *Women Who Run with the Wolves*.

WRITING ROMANCE IN THE 21ST CENTURY: PLOTTING AND PLANNING

"[Wild Woman's] home is that place in time where the spirit of women and the spirit of wolf meet — the place where the mind and instincts mingle, where a woman's deep life funds her mundane life. It is the point where the I and the Thou kiss, the place where, in all spirit, women run with the wolves."

- *Angry Young Man* — British playwright John Osborne's 1956 play *Look Back in Anger* spawned the term *angry young men* to describe Osborne and his generation of playwrights who wrote harshly realistic stories as a backlash against the previous generation's escapist theatre. This archetype sees injustices all around. Life is consumed with the need to rage at the darkness in life, seemingly blind to the light.
- *Passionate Archetypes: lover, rebel, artist, seeker* — This group of archetypes were labeled *The Soul Seekers* by Carl Jung, the founder of analytical psychiatry. Soul Seekers are strongly motivated, passionate perfectionists who are often deeply spiritual. They are able to love deeply but will also suffer deeply if they are forced to give up their art. Nora Roberts' novel *Born in Fire* and her novel *Dance to the Piper* both feature passionate artists as their feminine heroes.
- *Weary Warrior* — The weary warrior who was once a hero has become a cynical *anti-hero*, exhausted by battle. The award-winning movie *Casablanca* opens with a scene which portrays Rick as an embittered anti-hero hiding from the battles of World War II in Casablanca. At the end of the movie, transformed into a true hero by his love for Ilsa, the woman who was once his wartime sweetheart, Rick sacrifices a possible future with Ilsa, sending her away to safety with her husband, the renowned Czech resistance leader Victor Laslo. As the plane bearing Ilsa and Victor to safety flies away from Casablanca, Rick and his friend Renault are planning to join

a nearby free French garrison.
- *Earth mother* — The earth mother has a bottomless well of maternal love to give, nurturing simply by her presence. She is well grounded and seems unshakable. She is fulfilled by giving to children, partners, lovers, and friends. Her strength is quiet and certain. Earth mother also has a masculine counterpart, whose nurturing tends to be more concrete.
- *Virgin* — The virgin feels deeply, cares deeply about others, but may shy away from sexual intimacy. Virginal protagonists may be blind to their own passionate nature until awakened by love. A 21st century study of 7,589 adults aged 25 to 45 found that 2 percent of the women and 5 percent of the men had never had sex with a partner. This is from the article, *Are There Really 40-Year-Old Virgins?* Published in *Psychology Today* June 11, 2011) Significant factors in adult abstinence include profound shyness, social awkwardness, and general discomfort about physical intimacy. So, yes, your heroic protagonist might be a virgin.
- *Shapeshifter* — The shapeshifter archetype applies to any person who has a pattern of shifting appearance, mood, or behavior unexpectedly. Some shapeshifters undergo physical transformations, particularly in paranormal romances and urban fantasies. The masculine hero in Gail Crease's *Poseidon's Kiss* is the sea god Poseidon's son, shifting from underwater creature to human. In romances, this archetype often represents the mystery of a person of a different gender or sexual orientation who may appear bewilderingly confusing to others. This archetype is powerfully present in Meredith Russo's award-winning LGBT young adult romance *If I Was Your Girl*.
- *Shadow* — The shadow represents suppressed, hidden, or dark-side energies. Many romances feature dangerous shadow

WRITING ROMANCE IN THE 21ST CENTURY: PLOTTING AND PLANNING

heroes who are tamed or redeemed by love. Battles with the dark side have a strong primal appeal, evidenced by the enduring popularity of Emily Bronte's Heathcliff in *Wuthering Heights,* and the 21st century wave of vampire and werewolf heroes in paranormal romances. By their very nature, vampire and werewolf characters represent both shapeshifter and shadow archetypes.

Adding the power of romantic love to these archetypes has the potential to create deep moral dilemmas, driving character motivation and page-turning conflict. J. R. Ward's *Black Dagger Brotherhood* series and Patricia Briggs *Alpha and Omega* series are both excellent examples of both shadow and shapeshifter archetypes, and the power of love.

- *Trickster* — This mischievous archetype is present in all comic characters, and in characters who deliberately practice trickery, break the rules, and outwit others to get what they want. Raven and Coyote are both represented as tricksters in mythology. Con men, secret agents, detectives, and undercover police all practice trickster behavior. The actions of tricksters may produce either positive or negative outcomes.
- For more information about archetypes, see Christopher Vogler's *The Writer's Journey,* Joseph Campbell's *The Hero with a Thousand Faces*, and Carol S. Pearson's *Awakening the Heroes Within.*

THE ALPHA FEMALE

THIS TALENTED, SELF-confident, and highly motivated woman embraces her leadership ambitions and tends to:

- Believe her ability to achieve is limitless;

- Self-identify as an alpha female;
- Have a contagious confidence, which leads other to respect her as an equal;
- Showcase leadership characteristics;
- Be recognized by others as being impactful, and ...
- Have extremely high ambitions.

— *The Alpha Female: 9 Ways You Can Tell Who is an Alpha Woman.* <http://bit.ly/AlphaWoman>

THE ALPHA MALE

"When we speak of human alpha males today, it may be that we refer to the trait of social dominance: Studies have demonstrated that socially dominant men hold sway with many women and can invoke feelings of inferiority among men. Thanks to current research, these men may also be more readily identifiable."
— *Vinita Mehta Ph.D.*

SCIENTIFIC STUDIES have found that the following three physical features are strongly associated with male rankings of social dominance and leadership: height, tone of voice, and having a handsome or rugged face.

Taller men are perceived as more masculine, enjoy more leadership roles, have higher starting salaries, and show less jealousy toward their rivals in the western world, but studies have shown that this is not true in all cultures.

- Deeper voiced men are perceived as larger, stronger, heavier, older, and more dominant.
- A handsome and/or rugged male face is associated with male dominance.
- Researchers have found that men who have higher

WRITING ROMANCE IN THE 21ST CENTURY: PLOTTING AND PLANNING

testosterone exhibit [a more pronounced ratio of] facial width to facial height and are richer and more violent.

— *Are Alpha Males a Myth or a Reality?* http://bit.ly/TheAlphaMale

The 21st century romance author has a wide range of choice in characterizing an alpha male, ranging from the modern non-violent alpha whose leadership rests on social dominance, through warriors, whose way of life may include physical violence; for example, police, secret service agents, soldiers in battle — all the way to shapeshifting vampires and werewolves whose alpha dominance is highly physical, and may be filled with rage to the point where the alpha loses control.

Robyn Donald talks about
THE ALPHA HERO

WHY IS YOUR HERO SO tough, hard and outrageously masculine? You need to know, so that you understand what sent him down the Alpha road. What secret vulnerability is he hiding — especially from the heroine? An Alpha hero should directly threaten the heroine's peace of mind, her way of life, but never forget — he's a good man.

Show that he's a hero, with all that that implies — generosity of spirit, competence, confidence. Because he's a hero, he is never needlessly rude or aggressive.

A hero demands high standards. Although he's a natural leader, that inborn authority and control over his emotions have been honed by intelligence, experience, and circumstances. The writer needs to know what those circumstances were, or to discover them as she writes.

An Alpha hero tries to behave according to his own ideas of honor. If he fails, he has an over-riding reason for his treachery — often the greater good of mankind — for which he may feel he has to sacrifice both his own happiness and that of the heroine.

There's an aura of danger about the Alpha hero. This man lives by his own rules; he's strong-willed enough to impose those rules on others, but he has a healthy respect for humanity and its laws.

At first, he may not understand that the strong sexual attraction he feels for the heroine can be transmuted into love. He may begin by being cynical about emotions, but by the end of the book he's learned that he can trust the heroine with his happiness and honor. So he must have the capacity to love, to feel compassion, to learn to live with another person.

Robyn Donald *has almost seventy published romance books to her credit and is co-author of "Writing the Romantic Novel" by Daphne Clair and Robyn Donald.*

SUMMARY: POWERFUL ARCHETYPES FOR YOUR CHARACTERS

THROUGHOUT TIME, POWERFUL character archetypes appear again and again in human myths and stories. These myths, themes, and archetypes are a powerful tool for storytellers.

- *Wild Woman—* passionately and completely herself, never needs to wear a mask, and is certain of her identity.
- *Angry Young Man* — a term originally applied to a 1950s generation of British playwrights consumed with the need to rage at the darkness of life.
- *Passionate archetypes: lover, rebel, artist, seeker* — strongly motivated, passionate perfectionists who are often deeply spiritual. Psychologist Carl Young labelled this archetype *The Soul Seekers*.
- *Weary Warrior* — a cynical antihero, exhausted by battle.
- *Earth mother* — this archetype has a bottomless well of maternal love to give. This archetype has a masculine

counterpart, whose nurturing tends to be more concrete.
- *Virgin* — virginal characters may be blind to their own passionate nature until awakened by love. Significant factors in adult abstinence include profound shyness, social awkwardness, and general discomfort about physical intimacy.
- *Shape Shifter* — any person who has a pattern of changing appearance, mood, or behavior unexpectedly.
- *Shadow* — this archetype represents suppressed, hidden, or Darkside energies. Many romances feature shadow heroes who are tamed or redeemed by love.
- *Trickster* — this archetype is found in all comic characters, and in those who deliberately practice trickery, break the rules, and outwit others to get what they want.
- *Alpha* — the *alpha* character is a confident, dominant, impactful and ambitious leader. As Robyn Donald points out, a true, heroic alpha character should never be needlessly rude or aggressive.

Although archetypes may be specifically portrayed in mythology as male or female, the spirit of an archetype can inhabit any character.

4: Getting Ideas: the Story Spark

"The writer clearly requires ideas. Precious little gets written without them. In many types of writing, once a certain level of professional competence is granted, it is the strength or weakness of the idea itself which determines the success or failure of the finished piece of work. It is this absolute need for ideas which one generates oneself that makes the process of literary creation wholly incomprehensible to a great many people not engaged in it. The writer is not buying widgets from Mr. A and selling them to Mr. B. He is making something out of nothing, out of thin air. He is getting ideas, and it would seem to follow that he must be getting them somewhere."
— Lawrence Block, Telling Lies for Fun and Profit

STORY IDEAS COME FROM life, from the subconscious, from the creative part of the brain. Your stories can be sparked by things you hear, see, feel, or by your own stray thoughts.

WRITING ABOUT YOUR FEARS

WHEN YOU FEAR SOMETHING, your fear generates *What-if...* thoughts: What if the plane crashes? What if the dog bites? What if the boat sinks?

My novel *Wild Passage* was sparked by a terrifying experience at sea.

WRITING ROMANCE IN THE 21ST CENTURY: PLOTTING AND PLANNING

My husband Brian and I were cruising our 46-foot sailboat, *Julie Marie II,* from British Columbia's Pacific coast to San Francisco. Just as night fell on our third day at sea, the wind freshened. Suddenly, we were running south in six-foot seas with the wind behind us and a cross swell making steering hazardous.

We had to reduce sail, and quickly. Brian put me on the wheel, snapped a safety line onto his lifejacket, and went forward to reef the mainsail. While he was on deck reducing sail, a massive ocean swell humped up under the stern of the boat, swinging us off course.

I couldn't catch the wheel soon enough. The wind shoved the boom up under the flapping mainsail, slamming both sail and boom across the deck with an explosive crash.

My world veered to the starboard while I fought the wheel to stabilize the boat. I couldn't see Brian anywhere. Panic surged through my veins as *Julie Marie II* fought the chaotic seas. Where was my husband?

Even now, remembering that night, my chest tightens, breath frozen, heart racing in the echo of those frozen seconds while I struggle to stabilize the boat, my ears filled with the machine-gun chatter of our wind-ripped Canadian flag flying from the flagpole at the stern of the boat.

Brian? Where's Brian?

Finally, the boat steadied and under the boom of the sail, I spotted a flash of orange. Legs. Two legs. Brian. I couldn't spot his head, but his legs were upright. And his hands — Yes, his hands! Tying the sail's reef points down to the boom.

He was alive, still standing. Reefing the mainsail. Not thrown overboard to be towed through the wild seas by his own lifeline. Not lying on the deck, dying or dead from the impact of that flying boom.

Thank God!

Brian finished reefing the sail and took over the wheel. The boat was traveling easier under the reduced sail, keeping a steady course. We were safe, 70 miles offshore. *Julie Marie II* had just proved that she could handle the weather.

I ducked my head into the after cabin to check on our 13-year-old son Grant. He was in his bunk. Still sleeping. Our world was back to normal. We had made it, reefed the main, stabilized the boat, everything under control.

Everything except for my innards.

I opened the forward hatch and went down below to make us coffee. Inside, I took off my protective orange Mustang cruiser suit to be more comfortable, filled the kettle, and fired up our kerosene stove to boil water for coffee.

My heart was pounding. Stomach clenched. My jaw trembling. And my hands. Adrenaline, slopping around in my veins.

I sat down, feet on the floor under me, rocking, holding myself as if I held an infant.

What if...

What if I'm out here and Brian gets injured ... killed ... swept overboard in a gale and dragged by his lifeline? It's dark, there's a storm, no help except on the other end of a radio, the sea so wild we can hardly hear the coast guard reports on our radio warning mariners not to attempt to cross the river bars at the entrance to the only ports east of us.

Would I have the physical strength to reef the mainsail by myself in this weather, pulling it down against the pressure of the wind? I could call the coast guard, but rescues took time, and if those sandbars at the entrance to the harbor were closed, would the coast guard be able to cross them and get to us?

"It would make a great story," whispered a little voice in my mind.

That night became the spark for my novel *Wild Passage*.

WRITING ROMANCE IN THE 21ST CENTURY: PLOTTING AND PLANNING

Although I was no longer sure I could be the courageous adventurer I'd thought I was when we began the voyage, I fought my fears and we sailed on. Two days later we crossed the bar to Grays Harbor in calm waters, stayed for a few days, then sailed on to San Francisco where we met other sailors and shared stories with them.

In San Francisco, I let my fantasies loose in the world of fiction and *Wild Passage* was born. I gave my fears to a woman named Serena who signed on for a sailing adventure, only to discover the ocean had terrors she hadn't imagined.

I put Serena through the gale I had experienced, but more than that, I left her alone in the storm with an unconscious captain and no one but herself to control that 46-foot sailboat. She was terrified, but she knew she had no choice but to keep fighting.

In Serena, I created the heroic protagonist I hope I could have been in her place.

I had a wonderful time writing *Wild Passage,* and I loved using my own experiences at sea as an exciting background for Serena's journey into love.

What are you afraid of? Try dumping your character into your worst nightmare.

MYTHS AND FAIRY TALES

MYTHS, FAIRY TALES, and archetypes provide wonderful story sparks. The fairy tale *Cinderella* has been written again and again in romance: handsome prince falls in love with sweet, downtrodden peasant girl, showering her with love, happiness, and the wealth she truly deserves.

Well, it's not always like that. The 1998 movie *Ever After* tossed out the timid Cinderella, transforming her into a strong protagonist who guides her Prince Charming through transformational personal growth.

Maybe it's time to turn a fairy tale around. To swap the traditional roles. To have some fun.

REVERSING STEREOTYPES

MANY STORYTELLERS HAVE learned that turning stereotypes around can be fun. In my novel *Stray Lady,* I reversed the stereotype of the stay-at-home single mother teaching the rolling stone male the meaning of love and family.

It happened this way:

Georgina first appeared in my novel *Jenny's Turn.* She was Jenny's cousin, a guitar packing, rolling-stone widow cruising the North Pacific alone in the sailboat she and her late husband had bought before he died. By the time I'd finished writing *Jenny's Turn,* I knew I had to write George's love story, but how was I going to keep her in one place long enough to fall in love?

Then I thought of Green Island, a remote lighthouse island I had once lived on with my first husband. About a mile north of the lighthouse is Gray Island, little more than a rock covered with seaweed at high tide, a hazard to navigation.

Aha! Gray Island. Sailboat. Stormy weather. The perfect way to keep George in one place long enough to fall in love. Add one lighthouse keeper — Lyle, who had left his job as a seaplane pilot and taken the job of lighthouse keeper so he could keep his young daughter with him.

Looking for a story spark?

Pick a stereotype ... then change it, flip it, turn it around.

POPULAR FAVORITES AMONG ROMANCE READERS & WRITERS

WRITING ROMANCE IN THE 21ST CENTURY: PLOTTING AND PLANNING

- *The lovers reunited book* — Two people were once lovers, then something went wrong. Time has passed since their relationship failed. They meet again, but this time, more mature, they face and conquer the issues that separated them in the past. In *If You Loved Me*, my protagonist seeks out her high school lover because she needs his wilderness expertise to find her son. In *Seeing Stars*, my astronomer protagonist attends a high school reunion, then impulsively propositions the man who was once the high school bad boy.
- *The hidden-baby book* — This is a special case of the lovers reunited story. Protagonist and lover once had an affair, perhaps even married. After they separate, a child was born without the father's knowledge. If you're contemplating a hidden-baby romance, you'll need a good reason for concealing the pregnancy and birth from the father. Of my 35 books, two have used the hidden baby plot device: *Hidden Memories* and *Yesterday's Vows*. Once, I had the fun of helping another writer to brainstorm a book in which we flipped the hidden baby archetype and made it the woman who didn't know she was the mother of her lover's child.
- *The marriage of convenience book* — Two people marry, but not for love. The marriage of convenience creates a crucible forcing two people together as they fall uncomfortably in love. There are many reasons for two people to enter an arranged marriage: economic reasons, business reasons, for family reasons, to give a child a home. A contemporary marriage arrangement must work in the modern world, with believable motivation for both partners. In my novel *Think About Love* two people married to secure the future of her infant niece and his software empire.
- *The amnesia book* — A romance character who has amnesia has a special conflict. How can anyone enter into a new

relationship not knowing if there is a spouse waiting, forgotten behind the barrier of memory? This issue has been explored in many romance novels including Rebecca Daniels' *Rain Dance*, Annette Broadrick's *Mystery Wife*, Rebecca Winters' *She's My Mom*, and Garrett Leigh's *What Remains*, winner of the 2017 Bisexual Book Award for Romance.

- *The kidnap book* — The romance protagonist is abducted by, or abducts, their intended love partner in this stereotype romance. Although some kidnap romances become bestsellers, I avoid reading or watching stories in which abusers are portrayed as heroes. On the other hand, turning the romantic abduction stereotype around can be fun, as I describe in *Chapter 6: Character Driven Plotting*.
- *The woman in jeopardy book* — Mary Higgins Clark and Joy Fielding have made careers out of this plot, and many romantic suspense novels feature it. The heroine is in danger, usually from an unclear source. She doesn't know who her enemy is, she may even think she has imagined the danger. The hero may appear to be the enemy.

WHAT IF...

STORIES COME IN MANY different ways, but once the spark comes into a storyteller's mind, the next step is to ask, *What if...?* The following is an example of how my story *So Much for Dreams* grew.

During the summer of 1988, I was living in La Paz on the Mexican Baja peninsula with my family. We had berthed *Julie Marie II* in La Paz and were eager to explore the Baja. Our attempt to purchase a reliable used car for day trips was unsuccessful, so Brian stayed with the boat while I traveled north with two friends who were visiting family in Arizona, while I purchased a used car. My friends and I returned a week later, driving the elderly Oldsmobile I'd purchased.

WRITING ROMANCE IN THE 21ST CENTURY: PLOTTING AND PLANNING

The sun was unrelenting on the return trip, and the car's elderly radiator proved incapable of cooling both the engine and the air conditioner.

Even after we shut down the air conditioner, we needed to stop several times when the radiator boiled over. Luckily, we had several jugs of water in the trunk of the car. I wasn't worried. I was with friends, I'd been in Mexico long enough to get along in Spanish, and I knew the helpful good-nature of the Mexican people

But the part of my brain that loves playing with stories couldn't help speculating. *What if* ...

What if a woman were driving these mountain roads alone in an undependable car, unable to speak Spanish, not knowing the country? Driving an undependable car alone in a remote area of a country where you don't speak the language is a dangerous thing to do. If my fictional heroine were to do such a stupid thing, she would need a good reason to put herself at risk.

Perhaps she worked with young girls in trouble. One of her young charges might have disappeared into Mexico. What if my protagonist — I'll call her Dinah — gets a letter from this young girl who is pregnant, abandoned, living on the beach in La Paz, Mexico? She can't call the girl, there's no phone.

Around this time in my plotting journey, I heard from a writer friend who had received a battered letter from me in her mail, mysteriously delivered months after I sent it.

Yes, that could work. Dinah's young friend sent her letter, but it didn't arrive until weeks later. Wherever the girl was when she wrote the letter, she's not there now.

I brainstormed Dinah's background, deciding that she was actively helping young girls, that she'd come out of a traumatic childhood strong and involved in life. In contrast, I gave her a love partner who had responded to trauma by withdrawing from the world. I made Joe a drifter, living on his sailboat in Mexico, hiding from the pain of his past, with no intention of ever becoming involved again.

I began *So Much for Dreams* with Dinah driving her aging Oldsmobile up a Mexican mountain. I tossed Joe in her path and gave them a reason to travel together. By the time the initial problems of Dinah's car and her pregnant young friend were resolved, Joe and Dinah were facing a deeper conflict — her committed life versus his vow never to risk caring again.

SUMMARY: GETTING IDEAS

TRY BRAINSTORMING WITH yourself to get ideas. Think about ...

- 10 places you've been.
- 10 things you've done.
- 10 things you'd like to do.
- 10 personal problems you have trouble dealing with.
- 10 things you fear.
- 10 things you feel guilty about.

If you can only get two or three, make something up.

You've got a lifetime of story material in your lists: settings, occupations, events, motivations. Look at your fears. Have you overcome all your fears? I certainly haven't, but in my experience, forcing my characters to overcome *theirs* can be great fun, and wonderful therapy.

What are you afraid of? What do you feel guilty about? What's your favorite holiday location? Toss your protagonist into that location, give them one of your problems, and ask yourself, *What if...?*

WRITING ROMANCE IN THE 21ST CENTURY: PLOTTING AND PLANNING

It's okay if you tell lies here. This is your universe of make believe and you're the supreme director here.

5: Characters, Motivation, and Plotting

"It begins with a character, usually, and once he stands up on his feet and begins to move, all I can do is trot along behind him with a paper and pencil trying to keep up long enough to put down what he says and does."
— William Faulkner

THE CHARACTER DRIVEN STORY

TIMELESS ROMANCES FROM award-winning movies can be great for stimulating the storyteller's own imagination, and that fantasy *"What if..."* engine.

1. *The African Queen (1952):* When her missionary brother is killed and the African village that they lived in burned to the ground at the beginning of World War I, Rose Morley is forced to flee in a small steam launch piloted by rough-and-ready cynic Charlie Allnut. During the tortuous passage, Rose's rigid morality and Charlie's rough-and-ready personality battle each other in the cauldron of that small boat, brewing both love and wartime heroism.
2. *Titanic (1997):* Shortly after 17-year-old Rose boards the ill-fated *Titanic* with her domineering mother and cruel fiancé, she attempts suicide only to be rescued by Jack, an adventure-loving artist who teaches her what's important in life.
3. *Love, Actually (2003).* This multiple award-winning British romantic comedy explores the different aspects of love, following the heartfelt relationships of 9 interconnected couples. Hugh Grant plays the lead as the newly inaugurated, unmarried British Prime Minister who inappropriately falls for one of his household staffers. Liam Neeson is brilliant as the grieving widower, who is struggling to help Sam, his

depressed preteen stepson who has fallen hopelessly in love with the young daughter of a famous singer. This is one of my favorite romance movies, largely because of the skill, warmth, and authenticity with which the writers, actors, and direct ors bring the characters to life manifesting the many faces of love.
4. *Love, Simon (2018)* This award-winning movie is based on Becky Albertalli's award-winning novel *Simon vs. the Homo Sapiens Agenda*. Simon is a high school boy who is falling in love with a fellow student during an anonymous email correspondence. The story opens with one of Simon's classmate's discovery of the eMail correspondence, and subsequent blackmail relating to Simon and his correspondent being gay.

NO MATTER HOW I DESCRIBE each of these award-winning love films, I can't say more than a few words before I come to the living characters at the heart of each story.

Although authors can and do play God, deliberately dumping characters into uncomfortable situations, it is the characters themselves who control each powerful story, and who chose how to react when faced with the crises their authors throw in their paths.

Each of these award-winning movies illustrates the essence of character-driven plotting:

1. Take a strongly developed character;
2. dump them into an uncomfortable, even terrifying, situation with a unique love partner;
3. ... then see what happens.

VANESSA GRANT

Within the limits of the world the author creates, the fully developed memorable character has free will. Like living people, fictional characters write their own stories by reacting to events when they make decisions consistent with their personalities and history.

By their own nature, living characters shape their own stories.

THE STORY SPARK

THE STORY SPARK FOR Shakespeare's Hamlet might well have been the question: What if a man encountered his father's ghost and learned his father had been murdered?

If Shakespeare asked that question, he must immediately have followed it with others: What kind of man was the son? What about the ghost? The murderer? Did the son have a wife? A girlfriend? A mother? A pet dog? Friends? What were his relationships to these other people? Was he a fighter? A pacifist? A bookworm? What were his dreams, goals, and hang-ups?

Without answering these questions, Shakespeare could not have written Hamlet's story.

Naomi Horton talks about
CHARACTER MOTIVATION

MOTIVATION IS THE SECRET to great characterization, to great conflict, and to great emotional intensity.

Romance novel characters do not just appear in this world fully grown with no history, family, or life. Like real people, they've had things happen to them — good and bad — that affect who they are, what they think, how they see the world, how they react to other people. In short, it's what makes them tick.

What Makes these People Tick?

WRITING ROMANCE IN THE 21ST CENTURY: PLOTTING AND PLANNING

Your lovers should each have a powerful motivation driving them through your story: this is their *prime motivating force* (PMF). It will color their every thought and will affect their every move. For the sake of your story, this PMF will have stemmed from a single, dramatic event in the character's past — the *prime motivating event* (PME).

Create a realistic backstory for both hero and heroine before starting to write your book. This is for both you and the reader. Even though many of the background details you brainstorm won't make it into the book, they will give you the deep familiarity with your characters that is required to create *living characters*.

To create strong emotional intensity, make the PME and resulting PMF emotionally powerful. To create strong romantic and emotional conflict between your protagonist and their love interest, give them conflicting prime motivating forces.

Example

You have a hero who is fiercely driven to fight crime (PMF) because his family was murdered when he was a child (PME). That PMF leads him to work as an undercover cop, and he lives by lies — his job is to make criminals trust him, and then he uses that trust to bring them to justice. If you have him meet a heroine whose PMF is the opposite — a woman who hates lies and deception, and believes they are never justified — you will have emotional conflict. Especially if she discovers that, as part of his job, he's been lying to her. (This is the setup for *No Lies Between Us*, by Naomi Horton, Silhouette Desire, 1991).

PMEs and PMFs do not always have to be negative: if a man who was hurt in love and doesn't trust his heart falls in love with a woman whose PME and PMF have taught her there is nothing that the power of love can't heal, they will be in tremendous — and powerful — conflict.

Naomi Horton *is a RITA award-winning author who has published over two dozen romance novels and has presented at several writers' conferences.*

VANESTA GRANT

Taking Chances ...
THE RIGHT MAN FOR THE JOB

AFTER A REAL-LIFE FRIGHTENING night at sea provided the spark for my novel *Wild Passage,* the book almost wrote itself, but not all my story sparks are so cooperative. The IDEAS folder residing on my computer's hard drive is the burial ground for dozens of dead plots, characters, and story ideas.

Kidnap was one of those dead story sparks.

It all started with a romance novel I was reading at the time.

My husband Brian and I were walking while I spilled my frustration about a novel I'd been reading. The supposed *hero* was a barbarian who had decided his best courtship strategy was to *kidnap* the woman he claimed to love. Walking along the Prince Rupert waterfront with Brian, ranting about all the reasons this book did not work as a romance, I muttered, "Why aren't there any romances where the woman kidnaps the man! Perhaps I should write one!"

It was a ridiculous statement and I didn't mean it, but during the weeks that followed, I found myself playing with plot ideas, exploring whether I could flip the story to have the woman kidnap the man, while making it both believable and justifiable.

To write the story to my satisfaction, I needed both character motivation and a scenario the reader could buy into — not to mention a scenario that *I* could buy into — while keeping it romantic. I was probably never going to write the story, because the premise was crazy, but ... for some reason I ended up starting notes for the book.

WHAT IF A WOMAN KIDNAPPED A MAN?

WRITING ROMANCE IN THE 21ST CENTURY: PLOTTING AND PLANNING

THE ANSWER TO THAT question was a cluster of new questions: Why would she kidnap him? Who is she? Who are the people around her? What are her hopes, dreams, goals? What frightens her? What does she believe she's best at? Worst? What makes her uncomfortable?

I couldn't begin telling the story without knowing both lovers intimately. I would also need to know where they lived and what effect their setting had on them.

I played with setting the story on Canada's Pacific coast where I'd lived for years, using the coastal logging industry as a background. I created brothers and cousins for my female protagonist, added a family business, with my two potential lovers related by marriage.

I created a pile of notes and on the surface the story looked okay, although hardly exciting. Despite the kidnapping, the loving, and the complications, I didn't have the chemistry to craft a workable plot.

For some reason, I kept working on it.

All humans have history, hang-ups, and goals. They interact with each other and with their environment. Those actions have results. Fictional characters are no different. Without history, hang-ups, and goals, my characters can't come to life. But put the events together and when it works, I have not only a plot. I have a story.

Despite having worked out an entire plot for the kidnapping idea, my characters weren't willing to go through with it. They thought it was stupid and melodramatic, and so did I.

But the idea kept nagging at me.

PLOT FRUSTRATIONS!

UP TO THIS POINT, I had spent very little time thinking about my protagonist's character. I'd given her a name — Misty — but I didn't know if she had a dog or not, or whether she ate eggs or oatmeal for breakfast. Misty was nothing more than an inert placeholder who for some stupid reason wanted to kidnap a nameless man she was going to fall in love with.

The reader might never care about the dusty details of Misty's history, where she was born or whether she failed high-school French. But like all characters, she had the potential to become stubbornly uncooperative if I ignored her dreams and fears. If I piled up a breathless series of disasters for Misty without stopping to find out what she wanted, she would transform into a bull-headed hunk of cardboard — or a rebellious teenager.

After writing pages of plotting notes and the first two chapters of Misty's story, the story still felt *flat*. I had a family logging business, an abduction to keep Misty's nameless potential love partner from a business meeting, a handful of details, and a dead story.

Misty was only a cardboard character, and I couldn't bring her to life.

Finally, I gave up and put *Kidnap* aside, moving it to the *Ideas* folder of my computer's hard drive for the unlikely event that I might want to go back to it.

I turned my attention to getting things ready for our voyage from Canada to Mexico with our youngest son on *Julie Marie II*. My next book would be *Wild Passage,* which I wrote while we were cruising down the US coast.

BREATHING LIFE INTO THE STORY SPARK

I FINISHED WRITING *Wild Passage* while *Julie Marie II* was berthed at the San Diego Yacht Club on our cruise from Canada to Mexico. Serena and Neil had survived their fictional version of my true-life experience in an offshore gale and were falling in love.

WRITING ROMANCE IN THE 21ST CENTURY: PLOTTING AND PLANNING

The San Diego Yacht Club felt amazingly luxurious after our time at sea. Late at night, Brian and I would swim laps in the Club's open-air pool under a starry sky, followed by a lazy session soaking in the club's hot tub which was sheltered by a towering palm tree.

Inevitably, a fictional version of the San Diego Yacht Club worked its way into *Wild Passage*, disguised as a marina and shipyard owned by Neil's wealthy family, and managed by his older brother, Zeb. *Wild Passage* gave Neil and Serena their happy ending, but it left Neil's brother living in a fictitious mansion attached to a marina that had this amazing hot tub under a star-studded black sky.

Something clicked in that dark pool of my subconscious where I was beginning to realize my muse lived. I'd written Zeb as Neil's big brother, the man everyone turned to when in trouble. But as glorious as this wonderful hot pool was, as amazing it was to lie back and stare at the palm trees and the star-studded sky, I'd left big brother with all the work of fixing other people's problems, and none of the fun. But *what if*...

... and right there, under San Diego's starry sky and the massive palm tree, my shelved *Kidnap* project sprouted up and broke out of the IDEAS graveyard.

Zeb was serious, the family rock, looking after everyone but himself, but I tossed the logging business from *Kidnap* out. Throw out Misty, too. Despite her whimsical name, she'd refused to come to life for *Kidnap*.

I already had the shipyard on the San Diego waterfront that I'd created as the family business in *Wild Passage*, and Zeb living in a big, ornate house next door to the marina, like one of those mini-mansions on Vancouver's Marine Drive.

Ideas flooded my mind. Zeb would come for a solitary swim and session in the hot pool late each night, when everyone else was asleep. Steady, dependable, too serious, a creature of habit. He needed someone to shake him up.

That would be Misty, but not the too-serious Misty I'd visualized while working on *Kidnap*. Zeb needed a lover to shake him up, and I was having fun. Leaning back in the hot pool under the starry sky, I realized that back in Prince Rupert I'd tried to plot out *Kidnap* too early, before I knew my characters. I'd spent too much time on plot and not enough on characters. I'd been playing *writer as God*, just like the parent who unwisely pressures an artistic child into a corporate management job.

This was, as one of my writer friends would say, an *epiphaniacal* moment.

Until my characters came to life for me in my imagination, I wasn't going to get a good story. To bring my stories to life I needed to know my characters deeply. I needed to know their history, hang-ups, goals and dreams.

I said a big thank you to my inner muse and dove deeply into Zeb's life.

The plot began to evolve. I was playing with Zeb, trusting my subconscious to dream up the plot while I built a history and environment that made psychological sense for Zeb's personality.

I gave Zeb a twin brother, Barry, who was scheming to keep Zeb away from the family business's annual shareholders' meeting. Hmm, maybe Barry had something to do with the kidnapping. Or …

Yes!

Barry was capable of skullduggery. He was a schemer. Someone who might, perhaps, persuade a private detective to abduct his twin brother. Perhaps if I made Misty the detective …

First, I needed to know more about Zeb's life and more about Misty. One thing I knew for sure, *this* Misty wasn't going to be the boring woman I'd constructed for the original *Kidnap* plot.

The evolution of Zeb, Misty, and their love story *Taking Chances* became my map for character-driven plotting.

WRITING ROMANCE IN THE 21ST CENTURY: PLOTTING AND PLANNING

SUMMARY: CHARACTERS, MOTIVATION, AND PLOTTING

POPULAR ROMANCES HAVE well-motivated, relatable characters who experience challenging situations on their journey to love. For those well-motivated, relatable characters to spark powerful stories, they must come to life in the storyteller's and in the reader's minds.

One powerful tool for developing strongly motivated characters and generating story sparks is Naomi Horton's PME/PMF concept. Create a prime motivating event (PME) in the character's background, resulting in the prime motivating force (PMF) that drives this character's actions, attitudes, and decision—and in doing so, creates the plot. It's best if the lovers' PMEs and/or PMFs lead to challenges on their journey to love.

Whether you're a Plotter or a Panster, playing around with your characters' history and driving forces can help grow your characters into living people in the minds of both you and your readers.

6: Character Driven Plotting: Growing a Couple

TAKING CHANCES
Zebadiah John Turner

I WANTED ZEB TO BE a man accustomed to looking after everyone but himself, who secretly yearns for excitement in his life, but believes he can't have it because he's too busy being responsible for those around him. My first step in breathing life into this caregiver hero was to give him a full name — Zebadiah John Turner — and describe his personality.

Next, I outlined his base characteristics, placing him in terms of age, physical appearance, and culture, writing down details as they popped into my mind, brainstorming with my subconscious, my muse.

Going on instinct, I jotted down significant events for his past history, events consistent with the man I envisioned. My goal was to flesh out Zeb's basic background in a way that explained how he became the person he is; how he developed the personality I'd assigned him. The more real Zeb became for me, the more likely he would come to life for the reader.

There were things I needed to know to write this book: Why is Zeb always the one who looks after the rest of the family? Why does he yearn for adventure instead of having his own adventures?

I created a childhood for my hero that groomed him to be his family's caretaker, jotting down the notes in the table that follows.

Zebadiah John Turner

WRITING ROMANCE IN THE 21ST CENTURY: PLOTTING AND PLANNING

PERSONALITY AND DEVELOPMENT
Personality

ZEBADIAH JOHN TURNER is solid, dependable, tends to keep to a routine. He is a caregiver, the family rock, not easily pushed around. Financially successful, he secretly yearns for excitement in his life.

Basic Details and Characteristics

- Born in San Diego 40 years ago. Son of prominent San Diego shipyard owner
- Ethnicity/Culture: Caucasian, Anglo-Saxon
- Religion: Christened in the Methodist church
- Physical: Tidy brown medium-length hair, hazel eyes, six feet tall, broad shoulders, lean body with hidden strength

Development – Significant Factors and Events

- Brought up wealthy and groomed to take over family responsibilities.
- Oldest of three boys. His father sheltered his mother, who liked it that way. Zeb learned to do the same.
- Quit college to take over management of family business at the age of 20, when his father died.
- Took in his younger brother Neil's teenage son last year when the brother was having trouble with the kid (*Wild Passage*).
- Never married. He isn't sure why. Maybe too busy looking after the dependents he has.
- Life has always been serious for Zeb. I plan to give him some excitement.

BECAUSE PEOPLE OFTEN behave differently toward family than to employees, differently with friends than lovers, I decided to explore the relationships and roles in Zeb's life. In doing so, I created a cluster of characters that would flesh out Zeb's world.

Although some of the details in the previous table and the one that follows never got into the book, brainstorming them brought both Zeb and my story world to life in my mind.

Here are my notes.

Zebadiah John Turner
RELATIONSHIPS AND ROLES
Parents

- *Mother*: Zeb looks after his mother, bails her out of problems with resigned patience, picking up where his father left off. He does not expect her to think for herself.
- *Father* (deceased): Zeb looks after the business and the dependents his father left him. He's the patriarch of his family.

Siblings (2 brothers)

- *Barry* is Zeb's twin brother, born just after Zeb. He is divorced and constantly in trouble. Zeb makes sure Barry's abandoned wife and child are okay, looking after the financial and paternal responsibilities Barry neglects.
- *Neil*, 2 years younger. Zeb feels protective urges toward his younger brother, but Neil seldom accepts and usually does not need help. However, Zeb is currently making a home for Neil's son.

WRITING ROMANCE IN THE 21ST CENTURY: PLOTTING AND PLANNING

Nephews

- *Keith:* Neil's son Keith is presently living with Zeb, who takes time to be buddies with the boy. They have a good relationship that's loose but nurturing.
- *Justin* is Barry's son. Zeb keeps a watchful eye on Justin, because Barry doesn't.

Love Interests

- *Alice.* They've known each other all their lives. Friends with benefits. She relies on his business advice. For Zeb, Alice is a longtime friend, safe sex partner, and another emotional dependent.
- Sister-in-Law *Helen*, Barry's ex-wife. She calls Zeb whenever Barry's alimony check is late, or Justin needs glasses.

Family Business

THE FAMILY OWNED SHIPYARD and marina have been run efficiently by Zeb since his father's death. As a result, the whole family is getting richer in a conservative way.

Employees

Club waiter: Zeb keeps up on news about the man's family, new baby.

Zeb's unusual name

Zebadiah John: Zeb could dodge his unusual name by using *John*, but he doesn't. Doesn't dodge responsibility, either.

Activities

Zeb attends weddings, funerals, and family occasions.

THE RIGHT WOMAN FOR THE JOB

NOW THAT I KNEW ZEB so well, I was eager to give him a lover who would open his horizons and shake him up. I needed the right woman for the job.

I began with Misty's personality, creating her in contrast to Zeb. Where he was secure in personal and family relationships, but a stranger to adventure; I made her comfortable with danger, but uncomfortable in personal relationships.

Because he was so family oriented, I designed an unconventional partner for him, a woman who had never been looked after. Because his life was barren of excitement and adventure, I gave him a lover designed to shake him out of his sedate rut.

I gave Misty and Zeb a common cultural heritage. But where I'd given Zeb a physical appearance consistent with his personality, I made Misty a small, blonde woman who people tended to label as frivolous. I decided to make her a private detective, a profession that made an asset of people's tendency to underestimate her based on looks.

I needed something in Misty's origins to explain how she became a private detective, comfortable with danger and subterfuge, yet wary of personal relationships. The answer had to lie in the events of her early development.

Because differences between hero and heroine are excellent for creating complications and conflict elements, I decided that while Zeb knew everything about his family history, Misty knew almost nothing. *She was really coming to life for me now!*

I know from studying psychology that trauma and abandonment in the formative first six years of life can be difficult if not impossible to overcome, so I gave Misty a loving and secure home for the first six years of her life. I followed Misty's early secure environment with a tragic accident that killed her parents, putting her into the care of her alcoholic, private-detective uncle.

WRITING ROMANCE IN THE 21ST CENTURY: PLOTTING AND PLANNING

Yes, this was making sense. Misty's unconventional upbringing taught her not to rely on anyone, while her childhood apprenticeship in a detective agency trained her to be self-sufficient.

By this time, Misty and Zeb were coming alive for me as a couple, and plot ideas sparked in my brain. These were real people with real complications, challenges that could give solid "downstream" effects as the story moved along.

When I decided Misty didn't know *how* her parents had died, I realized they had been killed in a car accident, and that Uncle Kenny had been driving, drunk. This family secret provided mystery in Misty's background, and also reinforced her adult role as a professional who specializes in uncovering secrets.

Has Misty ever used her profession to find out what happened to her parents? No, I decided. Because she was afraid to find out, sensing her knowledge could destroy her relationship with her only relative, Uncle Kenny.

Here are my notes on Misty ...

Misty Donovan
PERSONALITY & DEVELOPMENT
Personality

MISTY DONOVAN IS INTELLIGENT and adventurous, enjoys danger and a challenge. She's confident in her job as a private detective, but insecure in personal relationships. Does not trust anyone to look after her, depends on her own judgment, and resents being pushed around. She's shattered when anything happens to the people she cares about. She knows how to handle other people's crises, but not her own.

Basic Details and Characteristics

- Born in northern United States 26 years ago.
- Race/culture: middle class Caucasian Anglo-Saxon

Protestant.
- Religion at birth: She doesn't know.
- Physical: Five feet, two inches tall, small, slender, very physically fit. Blonde naturally curly hair. People often mistake her for a lightweight blonde, a fact she uses in her work and believes she's learned not to resent.

Development – Significant Factors and Events

- Brought up well-loved and cared for until around age 5 or 6, when she was orphaned. Misty doesn't know what happened to her parents. Uncle Kenny, her only relative who took her in charge, never explained.
- Sent to boarding schools. Spent her summers living in Kenny's bachelor pad.
- She was 8 years old when she asked her uncle how her parents had died. He stormed out on a drunken bender and did not return for a week.
- After that, she saved her allowance and kept money and food stashed to feed herself if he disappeared again. She learned not to trust.
- From the age of 8, she spent most of her holidays hanging around her uncle's detective agency. She became skilled at following people, etc.
- She fell in love with a wealthy student while she was in college. He dumped her when he realized how unsuitable her background was (i.e., after he met Kenny).
- She went to work for her uncle after graduating, got her private detective's license, became his partner, and now she looks after him.

WRITING ROMANCE IN THE 21ST CENTURY: PLOTTING AND PLANNING

UNCLE KENNY IS THE most important person in Misty's present life. She loves him deeply, but fears losing him. This insecure relationship provides the background for Misty's other relationships and explains both her discomfort in personal relationships, and her comfort with dangerous situations.

Because Misty has so few intimate relationships, there was a danger the reader might find her cold and uncaring, so to show the reader Misty's capacity for love, I gave her a dog.

Misty Donovan
RELATIONSHIPS & ROLES
Parents

MISTY'S PARENTS died early in her life. Misty doesn't know how they died and is afraid to ask Uncle Kenny after that one attempt when she was 8.

Uncle Kenny

Uncle Kenny is Misty's only known relative. She loves him but does not trust him.

Kenny's alcoholism: Misty is silent about Kenny's benders and covers for him (Enabling behavior).

The Detective Agency

Misty learned to be a detective from Kenny, but she's been the backbone of the agency ever since she became his partner. She's good at pretend games and sleuthing, and — like many adult children of alcoholics — very skilled at reading people and atmospheres.

Employees

Jo-Anne: Misty and Kenny's secretary. Jo-Anne is an old-timer who knows the score, secretly loves Kenny, and wants romance for Misty.

Lovers

Wayne: Misty fell in love with Wayne in college, did everything she could to be what he wanted, to play the right role, but it wasn't enough. Her relationship with Wayne taught her not to try to fit where she doesn't belong.

Vehicle

Her Corvette: Fast and exciting. Misty loves her car.

Misty's Dog

Misty rescued Max, an abandoned Doberman Pinscher. He barks at shadows, paper bags, and strangers, and gives Misty the only unconditional love she has. Max is probably the only creature Misty truly trusts. She bought her house to give Max a home.

BACKSTORY & MOTIVATION

WHEN I DEVELOP MY CHARACTERS, fleshing out their backstories and environment, I'm constantly working to understand what motivates this person.

Why does Zeb always look after his family? Why hasn't he married? Why doesn't Misty trust anyone to look after her? Why did Kenny get drunk when Misty mentioned her parents?

As human beings, our actions and patterns can often be explained by events in our past. Sometimes a single event provides powerful motivation. As I discussed in Chapter 5, author Naomi Horton calls an incident like this a *prime motivating event (PME)*.

Our human brains process events that happen in early childhood and throughout our lives, automatically assigning them meanings. These assigned meanings evolve into a system of *core beliefs* that are programmed into the brain, largely unconsciously, influencing our emotions, our beliefs, and our reactions. The nature of these core beliefs determines our *prime motivating forces (PMFs)*.

WRITING ROMANCE IN THE 21ST CENTURY: PLOTTING AND PLANNING

After a prime motivating event occurs, subsequent experiences may reinforce it. If a woman's father abandons the family when she's a child (prime motivating event), the child may believe daddy doesn't love her. Years later, when her high school boyfriend breaks up with her, emotions and pain from childhood surge to the surface, reinforcing the prime motivating event and bumping up her earlier belief that '*daddy doesn't love me*' to an entrenched core belief that '*I'm unlovable*.'

When your characters' personalities and prime motivating forces develop from realistic prime motivating events and core beliefs, your readers will unconsciously recognize these patterns and perceive your characters as *real people*.

Misty's prime motivating force is a need to be independent, based on distrust. She learned not to count on people when her parents disappeared (prime motivating event). When she was eight, her uncle reinforced that distrust by disappearing and leaving her alone for a week. At college, her lover Wayne reinforced her distrust again.

Zeb's prime motivating force is a need to look after people. He was trained to it early, and then the motivating event of his father's death threw him deep into his Mr. Responsibility role. All the relationships around him reinforce that role.

Prime motivating events trigger prime motivating forces that can be positive, negative, or both. Misty's prime motivating force of independence and distrust is a barrier to intimacy, but the circumstances that created her distrust also made her strong, resilient, and an excellent detective.

PUTTING CHARACTERS TOGETHER

ZEB AND MISTY'S CHARACTERS, histories, hang-ups, and goals make certain things inevitable when they get together.

- Zeb is going to want to look after Misty. It's as natural as

breathing to him.
- Misty doesn't trust anyone to look after her.
- This conflict between their goals will cause trouble.
- Once Zeb falls in love, he's going to want marriage and children.
- Misty knows she can't fit into the world of the wealthy and stuffy. Even Zeb's house frightens her.
- This conflict between their goals will cause trouble.

I decided to use the title *Taking Chances,* because, prior to meeting Misty, Zeb has avoided taking chances. Misty was willing to take chances everywhere except in her private life.

With my central characters fleshed out, my plan was to start the story at the detective agency with Zeb's twin brother Barry tricking Misty into helping him abduct Zeb. However, when I began writing that scene, I almost immediately came into conflict with the character I'd created.

Misty was nobody's fool. She'd grown up on lies and evasions. No matter how good a con Barry presented, she would see through it. Yes, she would!

My characters had an answer for that. Under the guidance of Misty, Zeb, and Barry, I began writing ...

Taking Chances: Chapter One

Misty pushed the button two minutes after Zebadiah Turner sat down in the uncomfortable chair by the window. It was simply instinct.

She sat down when he did. She crossed her legs and adjusted her pleated skirt smoothly to avoid showing her knees. She leaned back in her chair and waited to see if he would speak first. She knew the image she projected; small and blonde and fluffy. All her life men had been underestimating her because of her tiny good looks. She had learned not to resent it. In her line of work, it was an advantage to have hidden skills.

WRITING ROMANCE IN THE 21ST CENTURY: PLOTTING AND PLANNING

WHEN I CONSIGN A STORY idea to my IDEAS folder, I rarely return to resurrect it, but *Kidnap* was different from the beginning. The original story spark was outrageous and born in anger over a book I considered offensive. It was frustrating in the beginning, but once I stopped trying to "think" the book into life and let my subconscious play around with it, I had a terrific time writing *Taking Chances*. That book taught me more about characters and plotting than any other book I'd previously written.

CHARACTER CHECKLIST

- Do your characters fit the story spark?
- Are they alive? Do you care about them?
- What do these people want?
- Why can't they have it?
- Should they have it?
- What happens when goal meets obstacle?
- What then?
- What doesn't work about this whole thing?
- When it REALLY doesn't work, try throwing out your character, the story spark, or the setting and bringing in something new!

SUMMARY: PLOT GERMINATION REQUIREMENTS
THE AUTHOR NEEDS ...

- A story spark with believable characters

Believable characters need ...

- Personality
- Abilities and disabilities
- History, hang-ups, and goals
- Relationships to career, house, city, weather, traffic, etc.
- Relationships (past and present) to friends, family, lovers, and pets
- Prime Motivating Events (PMEs) and Prime Motivating Forces (PMFs)

Your story needs ...

- A plot goal (i.e., your lovers achieve true partnership)
- An opening conflict or problem to get things started
- Living characters with goals, forced to face a difficult situation
- Obstacles between characters and their goals
- A setting, and characters with attitudes to the setting

**If something doesn't work – change it!
You are the Creator!**

"If you try to force inspiration, you will strangle it and achieve much less overall. There may be 'on' days and 'off' days, or even 'on' hours and \off hours. If you don't feel inspired, that's fine, go out and enjoy yourself. Your boss may disagree, but it's probably the most productive thing you could do. If you can, try not to have a boss." — Neel Burton MD: Psychology Today. How to Find Inspiration.

7: More About Characters

"When writing a novel a writer should create living people; people not characters. A character is a caricature." — Ernest Hemmingway, Death in the Afternoon

WOUNDED CHARACTERS AND HEAVY BAGGAGE
YOU NEED CHARACTERS with strong personalities — characters real enough to have both strengths and weaknesses. In developing these characters, you'll give them problems, failures and victories, and some emotional baggage to carry into the story.

Some years ago, I began writing a book called *Going Home*, about a woman named Annie who gave up her newborn child for adoption because of fear she might harm the child. She then ran away to Mexico to live.

Annie yearned for her child and for the home she'd never had. Distrustful and wounded, she blocked relationships from her life, except one relationship with a neighboring Mexican boy. In the course of the story, Annie would return to build a relationship with the daughter she'd given up and to find love.

Although my beta readers who read Going Home were moved by Annie and her daughter Jenny, and my new agent was enthusiastic, I couldn't find a publisher for the book.

It took a perceptive critic to point out that for most of the story Annie is a victim, weighed down by old pain and grief. Instead of taking charge of her own life, she was merely reacting to the events I'd written for her.

Annie needed to be proactive. It didn't matter if she made mistakes, but she must be active in determining her own fate. One day I may try writing Annie's story again. If so, I'll write about a wounded woman whose actions provide the catalyst for events in the story. She'll make mistakes, but she'll win her happy ending with her own strong efforts.

Whatever your characters' baggage, it's important that it doesn't weigh them down to the point of being passive. In my novel *Taking Chances*, Misty is distrustful and determined to be independent while Zeb secretly yearns for adventure. Neither one of them is helpless. They are active, heroic, living characters, making decisions that have downstream consequences for the story.

If Misty were so distrustful of others that she was incapable of fantasizing a relationship with Zeb, it would be much more difficult to write the romance.

YOUR BEST FRIENDS AS CHARACTERS

YOUR BEST FRIEND'S name is Constance and you want to write her into your romance novel. The idea excites you, and of course Constance will be thrilled.

Inevitably, if you've created strong, believable characters in a real-life conflict, those characters will surprise you. The characters may change and shift, and as the creator of this story, your job is to watch and try to understand the changes. Then, when the characters and the story require it, respond by being willing to recreate your living characters to grow a better story.

Real live characters have good moods and bad moods, both positive and negative personality characteristics. The problem here is that the inner critic sitting on your shoulder while you write knows that your vision of Constance is going to be published for the world to see.

WRITING ROMANCE IN THE 21ST CENTURY: PLOTTING AND PLANNING

Whether or not you're aware of it, your relationship with Constance will sanitize your portrayal of her, making your story less powerful than it might otherwise be.

As a writer, you can't afford to worry what your characters will think of you.

USING REAL PEOPLE CREATIVELY

DO YOU STILL FEEL A yearning to slip Constance into your book? When you look at her, do you see a beautiful, talented woman who is inexplicably alone? Are you hungry to do something about that evocative loneliness?

Does your creative mind play with the question: What if a beautiful woman, happily living alone, one day meets a man who makes her yearn for marriage and romance?

To develop this story to its full potential, you must be willing to abandon the real Constance. You must be free to change her name to Barbara or Janet or Kimchi, allowing her to transform herself and rebuild her history to explain that dedicated loneliness.

When she finds herself attracted to the man you've designed for her, you don't want to be hampered by a real-life Constance looking over your shoulder, judging your fictional character against her own standards.

Without Constance looking over your shoulder, you're free to name your heroine Kimchi and give her the free will to go wherever your imagination leads, giving you permission to throw whatever obstacles you want in the path of Kimchi's love story.

Kimchi is unlikely to have any resemblance to the real Constance. She's the product of your imagination, sparked by the question: *"What if...?"*

VANESSA GRANT

"THE 17TH-CENTURY PHILOSOPHER John Locke suggested that inspiration amounts to a somewhat random association of ideas and sudden unison of thought. If something, anything, catches your interest, try to follow it through. Nothing is too small or irrelevant. Read books, watch documentaries, visit museums and exhibitions, walk in gardens and nature, talk to inspired and inspiring people . . . Feed your unconscious." — Neel Burton MD: Psychology Today. *"How to Find Inspiration"*

TECHNIQUES FOR GETTING TO KNOW YOUR CHARACTERS

YOUR MALE PROTAGONIST is determined never to fall under his ex-lover's spell again.

Why is that? To write a real page-turner, you must know your characters intimately. You must know the answers to a universe of questions about this person: What motivates him? What motivated his ex-lover to drive him away? How can you flesh them out into real people?

Sometimes your characters' motivations and histories may emerge full grown in your mind. At other times, it's as if a curtain were dropped between the author and the creation.

How can you pull that curtain aside?

The Character Journal ...

Author Naomi Horton once told me she'd had a problem with her hero, so she sat down and let him tell her the answer — writing in first person. I borrowed her technique some time later when I was developing my thriller, *Rachel's Gun.*

One of my characters had left New Jersey and taken to the road with his motorcycle. I knew he was running from something. I knew he would meet my female protagonist and something about her would force him to stop, to engage with life instead of running away.

WRITING ROMANCE IN THE 21ST CENTURY: PLOTTING AND PLANNING

The problem was, I hadn't a clue what he was running from. Everything hinged on what had happened to the hero in New Jersey but whenever I asked myself, "What happened in New Jersey?" my answers seemed artificial, stilted, and unbelievable.

So, I sat down at my computer, opened a new, empty file, and began writing in first person. I told myself it didn't matter what I wrote, this wasn't part of the book, no one was ever going to see it, and I began by writing, "My name is Devin..."

I kept typing, although I had nothing to say...

MY NAME IS DEVIN. I had a regular woman once. That was a long time ago. Another life. I'm not going back. There's nothing to go back for. The myths have exploded.

AS I TYPED, DEVIN'S past came to life for me. Through some unknown magic, putting myself into the first person, actually typing *"My name is Devin..."* got me into his skin in a way my usual techniques couldn't. As I typed, my subconscious told me what he was running from, why he couldn't go back.

If you're stuck, try writing your character's journal for the day before your story begins. Then write the journal from a significant day when this person was 12 or 13 years old, an age at which most of us show strong signs of the adults we will become.

BRAINSTORMING A CHARACTER ...

WHILE STRUGGLING TO understand the protagonist of my women's fiction novel, *Lifelines: Kate's Story*, I taped large sheets of flip chart paper on my walls. Then, using a marking pen, I wrote headings on each sheet:

- 10 things Kate fears
- 10 things Kate loves
- 10 people Kate loves
- 10 people Kate would rather avoid
- 10 dreams Kate wishes would come true
- 10 situations Kate feels comfortable in
- 10 situations Kate feels uncomfortable in
- 10 things Kate likes about herself
- 10 things Kate dislikes about herself
- 10 things Kate regrets
- 10 memories Kate treasures

I wrote lists under each heading, wandering from one sheet to the another. The first couple of list items came easily, but by the time I reached number six, it was difficult to think of anything to add, but this is exactly when I knew I needed to continue, so I put down outrageous ideas until I got to number 10.

By the time I had spent an hour with my flip chart paper lists, the ludicrous ideas that I jotted down after I had run out of ideas shook my rigid brain into more creative paths and revealed my character's secrets.

Only then was I able to move to my computer and write Kate's character description and her journal, capturing the new ideas bubbling in my imagination.

E C Sheedy talks about ...
THE CHARACTER INTERVIEW

WRITING ROMANCE IN THE 21ST CENTURY: PLOTTING AND PLANNING

CHARACTERS ARE THE heartbeat of our stories. Sadly, they often refuse to jump, fully formed, into Chapter 1. It's up to us to bring them to life on the page, with a past logical enough to make their romantic present believable and compelling. If you're stuck on character development, one fun way of kick starting your muse is to get into your character's head — much like an actor does for a role.

How?

- Ask a friend to be your interviewer. A writer friend is best. They'll understand what you're trying to do.
- Record the interview. Recording will eliminate the distraction of taking notes.
- Give your interviewer a starter list of questions, then tell him or her to wing it, ask anything at all.
- Slip into character and answer all questions in the first person.

IF YOU'RE HAVING TROUBLE coming up with questions, here are a few suggestions:

- Where and when were you born?
- Tell me about your parents.
- Was your family rich, poor, or middle class? How did this affect you?

- Which parent were you closest to? What's your relationship today?
- Any siblings? Tell me about them. What's your relationship today?
- What's your educational background?
- Did you like school? If not, why not?

- Did you have a pet?
- Ever been married? What happened?
- What do you consider your best physical feature?
- Do you read? What kind of reading? Books? Magazines? Newspapers?
- What makes you angry?
- What do you care about most?

E C Sheedy is a multi-published romance, romantic suspense, and paranormal author.

SUMMARY: MORE ABOUT CHARACTERS

STORYTELLERS USE A variety of methods to bring their characters to life.

Think about the people you admire; the ones you dislike; and the ones that you're curious about. Think about the crazy situations you've seen people get into; things you've heard on the news or read in social media. There is a wealth of inspiration here to spark your creativity, grow your characters, and get story ideas.

Try experimenting with different methods to stir your creativity and breathe life into your characters. Here are just a few mentioned in this chapter:

- Naomi Horton's technique of journalizing a character in the first person
- Character brainstorming: making quick unfiltered lists of "10 things character likes, dislikes, fears, etc."
- E C Sheedy's technique of interviewing your character.

WRITING ROMANCE IN THE 21ST CENTURY: PLOTTING AND PLANNING

Whatever your character's weaknesses, strengths, and emotional baggage, your reader needs to know that this person's actions have power over the outcome of the story, and that by the end of the story, they will have experienced personal growth through their own actions.

8: Conflict & Struggle

"Light is meaningful only in relation to darkness, and truth presupposes error. It is these mingled opposites which people our life, which make it pungent, intoxicating. We only exist in terms of this conflict, in the zone where black and white clash." — Louis Aragon

INTERNAL vs. EXTERNAL CONFLICT

WHENEVER YOUR CHARACTERS struggle, they experience conflict. Characters, like human beings, experience both *internal* and *external* conflict.

INTERNAL CONFLICT is an individual's internal struggle over two or more goals. It's hidden from witnesses. Your characters need internal conflict.

In *Hidden Memories,* my protagonist Abby has a secret. Everyone believes her daughter Trish is her late husband's child, but Abby's daughter was conceived as the result of a night spent with Ryan, a man she encountered when she was in shock after her husband's death.

She knows she should be honest about her daughter's origins but telling the truth could hurt everyone around her if she acts: her daughter, her daughter's father, her late husband's father, and Abby's own parents.

When a character experiencing internal conflict acts out of that struggle, the struggle becomes externalized, creating conflict with other characters.

WRITING ROMANCE IN THE 21ST CENTURY: PLOTTING AND PLANNING

EXTERNAL CONFLICT is the struggle between people over opposing goals. External conflict is out in the open. It's visible to witnesses.

Ryan can't believe his eyes when he walks into an art exhibit and recognizes the woman he's never been able to forget. He's been obsessed by Abby's memory ever since she disappeared within hours of their first, *and only,* meeting. He's been searching for her for years.

Now he's determined to find out everything he can about her.

Abby's goal is to keep her secret. When she interacts with Ryan, who opposes that goal, that's external conflict. When characters with opposing goals interact with each other, those transactions reveal the external conflict between them.

When Abby sees her child's father across a crowded room, she tries to hide from him. Ryan could expose her secret, traumatize her daughter, and throw her life into turmoil.

Even before she makes the first move in her struggle with Ryan, before there's any evidence of external conflict between Abby and Ryan, her level of internal conflict has risen sky high. She's struggling with her conscience, Ryan's right to know he has a child, and her desire to avoid the unpleasantness that will result if her secret is exposed. Her mind is a buzzing cluster of stressful apprehension ...

- *Can I get out of here before he sees me?*
- *Does he know I'm here?*
- *What if he finds out about Trish?*
- *What— if he tries to take Trish from me?*
- *How can I explain this to my mother? She'll be so disappointed in me.*
- *What about Trish's grandfather? He'll never forgive me. He'll turn away from Trish.*

VANESSA GRANT

*Ryan's Obsession + Abby's Secret
= External Conflict*

THE TANGLE OF CONFLICT

IF YOUR CHARACTERS don't experience internal conflict, your readers won't believe that the issues in your story are important enough to worry about. Internal conflict drives external conflict, moving your story forward, creating the kind of anxiety and suspense that keeps readers up late at night turning pages.

Ryan and Abby have conflicting goals. Every step in the external struggle between them makes Abby's internal conflict worse.

Ryan wants to know why Abby disappeared after their one-night affair. Because of Abby's internal conflict, when the external struggle begins, her reactions are instinctive, not logical. She's under stress, attacked from outside by Ryan, from inside by her own conscience. She tries to hide, to pretend, to evade. Ryan becomes suspicious. Abby's mother likes Ryan and unknowingly makes the situation worse by throwing them together.

The increasing struggle between Ryan and Abby's opposing goals heightens the tension for Ryan, for Abby, and for the reader.

The stakes rise. The reader fears it won't work out for these people. Abby's apparent inability to live openly with the truth may drive Ryan away. Ryan may become angry and leave. The more uncertainty readers feel over the outcome, the more satisfied they'll be when these two lovers come together in the end.

WITH STRINGS ATTACHED

WRITING ROMANCE IN THE 21ST CENTURY: PLOTTING AND PLANNING

IN MY NOVEL *With Strings attached,* my protagonist Molly has a lifelong internal conflict regarding her father, so when he gives her a cabin on Gabriola Island, past history makes her fear that his gift has invisible strings attached. She loves him and wants to believe he loves her too but knows that he invariably lets her down.

The story opens with Molly driving across Canada to get to Gabriola Island on Canada's west coast, worried because her father's gift has intensified both her hopes and her fears.

Molly is secretly ashamed of her father. He's charming, fun loving, and an amazing artist. But he can also be irresponsible and shockingly manipulative. Her shame, her love, and her loyalty create an internal tangle of emotions.

When I wrote *With Strings Attached,* I could have tried to write a book in which Molly falls in love with Patrick yet can't trust him because she's been let down so often by her father. This sort of internal conflict could make it hard for any woman to have a successful relationship, but although internal conflict is necessary to a good story, it's not enough.

I need both *external* conflict, which makes the internal conflict worse, and *internal* conflict, which intensifies the *external* battle.

To create this tangle, I upped the stakes by making my male lover, Patrick, a public figure. Molly is attracted to Patrick, but when she learns that he's being courted by his political party, she's torn between her growing love for Patrick and the danger that her father's propensity for scandal represents, intensifying her *internal conflict*.

Molly begins to avoid Patrick, which ends up creating *external conflict* between them. He pursues her harder, intensifying that external conflict, and the closer they come, the more intense Molly's internal conflict grows.

To prevent what Molly sees as inevitable disaster, she tries to draw away from Patrick, heightening the external conflict.

At this point I up the stakes with a couple of transactions between Molly and her father that lead her to suspect he's up to something that's about to explode. She's now experiencing internal and external conflicts with both her father and Patrick. Afraid of the impact when her father's plot inevitably blows up, and to protect Patrick, she opposes his pursuit of her more strongly.

But Patrick won't stay away, and her father's public scandal explodes. The external conflict — trouble from her father and relationship aggression from Patrick — makes her internal conflict unbearable.

Molly flees from her lover, her father's mess, and the new life she craves. Her flight is an external conflict transaction, a nonverbal message Patrick interprets as rejection. He pursues her regardless and she throws nasty words at him to get free.

More external conflict. Molly and Patrick are both miserable. The misery is internal. The actions are external.

- *The internal conflict:* Molly's love for her father tangled with fear of his betrayals — makes the external conflict worse.
- *The external conflict transactions:* Patrick's uncomfortable pursuit of Molly despite her need for caution and her father's impending disaster — make the internal conflict worse

THE CONFLICT OF LOVE

THE MAGIC PROCESS OF two unique people coming together to form a bond of enduring love inevitably involves adjustments. Each person has a network of core beliefs, motivations, goals, and internal conflicts developed over a lifetime. Love is the magic force that can provide the motivation to overcome the inevitable differences and enable lovers to form lifetime bonds.

WRITING ROMANCE IN THE 21ST CENTURY: PLOTTING AND PLANNING

As your story progresses, your conflict must change and evolve. Because your lovers are human, they must struggle and make personal sacrifices to resolve both their internal and external conflicts.

Falling in love inevitably produces both internal and external conflict. We hurt the people we love. They hurt us. To have a successful relationship, both lovers must become vulnerable to each other, knowing that the other will sometimes hurt them, but trusting the relationship will be worth it.

In a love story, the conflict eventually develops to the point where the reader asks: "Do these two people care enough about each other to make the necessary compromises? Will they put their relationship above these other problems? Can they trust each other enough to become vulnerable, revealing their inner selves and committing to a lasting relationship in which the reader can believe? What will happen if they can't make it work?"

OPENING VERSUS DEVELOPING CONFLICT

ALL GOOD STORIES BEGIN with some sort of conflict, either internal or external. The conflict at the beginning of your book may or may not be related to the core conflict that unfolds as the story goes on. The opening conflict's real purpose is to keep the reader interested while you, as author, introduce characters and begin to show the bigger struggle that drives your story. The opening conflict need not be deep, although it may be, but it must feel real and it should tell the reader something about the character on stage.

In *Hidden Memories,* I opened with the primary internal conflict of my story, having Abby spot the one man in the world who could expose her lie about her daughter's parentage. When Ryan discovers Abby's lie, the external conflict issues change. Now Abby and Ryan are struggling over Ryan's access to their daughter. They're also struggling between

Abby's fear of committing to another relationship after her disastrous first marriage, and Ryan's desire to have a family relationship with both Abby and Trish.

In *With Strings Attached,* I opened with the heroine in a state of internal conflict, rushing to get to the cabin her father gave to her before the cat he abandoned inside the cottage dies of hunger.

The opening conflict needn't be earth shattering, but it should be immediate. If the book opens with the character in a state of internal conflict, this should lead to external conflict. To keep the reader turning pages, that opening conflict should not be resolved until the characters have other immediate problems.

ADVERSITY AND CONFLICT

YOUR CHARACTER MAY experience adversity — a traffic accident, a plane crash, a rainstorm destroying the sophisticated dress chosen for an important event. Each of these may cause severe problems, and although adversity is definitely bad luck, and it may trigger conflict, adversity itself is *not* conflict. Here's why:

Readers need to know that characters' actions matter, but characters and humans alike (unless they're magical) are powerless to change adversity. They do, however, have the power to choose HOW THEY RESPOND to adversity.

Adversity increases the tension in a story, causing detours in the path towards your characters' goals and increasing stress. Because adversity makes life more difficult, it has the potential to make problems for characters by ...

• forcing a change in the path characters take toward their goals
• making both internal and external conflicts more intense
• presenting life and death situations that overshadow previous goals

WRITING ROMANCE IN THE 21ST CENTURY: PLOTTING AND PLANNING

HOW TO CREATE CONFLICT

CONFLICT IS CREATED when goals meet obstacles. To create conflict, first give your character a goal, then have someone oppose that goal.

In *Hidden Memories,* Abby's goal is to keep the secret of her child's birth. Ryan opposes that goal, first discovering her secret, then making it impossible for her to keep it.

In *With Strings Attached,* Molly's goal is to avoid relationships in which her father's scandals could hurt her. Patrick unknowingly opposes that goal by pursuing Molly and falling in love with her, while being a public figure. Molly's father adds to the problem when he dumps Molly into a tax-evasion scandal.

To create conflict in your novel, give your character a goal with a high level of internal conflict, then have another character oppose that goal.

COMMON GOALS AND RELATED CONFLICTS
Goal: A Strong and Lasting Relationship

IN A ROMANCE NOVEL, whether the lovers realize it or not, their mutual story goal is to achieve a strong and lasting relationship with each other.

Internal conflict occurs whenever a person forms strong emotional bonds. We all fear betrayal, being hurt, not being lovable enough for the other person. Somewhere in your story, these fears will be present for each of your lovers.

External conflict results when differences between lovers threaten their goal of emotional love. It's important for each lover to struggle with the external results of their internal conflicts regarding the relationship. One lover may have difficulty allowing the vulnerability of love, and trusting their partner won't carelessly or deliberately hurt them. In response, the other may feel pain and anger when they sense signs of the other's distrust.

Goal: Keeping or Winning Possessions

INTERNAL CONFLICT occurs when a character worries about getting or keeping the desired house, car, business, or job, or struggles over whether the sought-after goal is the right one.

External conflict occurs when character A makes it difficult for character B to obtain coveted possessions or threatens to take something B owns. In response to the aggressive external conflict transaction, B must either fight, retreat, or reach a compromise.

Goal: Keeping Secrets

INTERNAL CONFLICT reveals itself to the reader when a viewpoint character's desire to believe they are a good person is challenged by the realization that they have morally transgressed. *Cognitive dissonance* is the discomfort our brains experience when struggling to resolve two conflicting beliefs. A brain experiencing *cognitive dissonance* will continue to be in distress until it either resolves or rationalizes the dichotomy.

When people feel guilty about transgressions, the process can last for a lifetime. In *Hidden Memories,* for years Abby has struggled to persuade herself that hiding the truth about her daughter's parentage is justified, and that it's the best thing for everyone concerned. That inner conflict drives much of the external conflict that occurs between Abby and Ryan, and between Abby and other members of her family. As humans, our characters experience personal growth when they resolve internal conflicts over morality.

External conflict occurs when the viewpoint character responds against actions or goals of other characters that threaten the viewpoint character's internal rationalization; or when they fear their moral transgression will be exposed. The more drastic the consequences of exposure, the more intense the conflict will be.

Goal: Gaining Achievements

INTERNAL CONFLICT develops because our human sense of self-worth is often tied up in our ability to achieve goals. For example, a person may have an intense desire to be a successful author, but fear they lack the talent, or that the relationship may fail if they become more successful, or less successful, than their love partner.

External conflict results when the people around the viewpoint character interfere with that character's goal. An editor may insist the character make extensive changes in the story. One writer's lover may complain when the writer spends too much time on the computer. With each cycle of internal and external conflict, the story is driven further towards a crisis and its final resolution.

Goal: Territory

INTERNAL CONFLICT occurs whenever we establish territory, or worry about what we'll do if someone else takes our personal territory. Personal territory could be anything we attach the word *"my"* to — my children, my home, my money, my job, or my self-respect.

External conflict occurs when territory is attacked, or we defend territory in response to real or imagined invasions.

In Chapter 10 I'll explore territory more deeply as a tool for developing story conflict.

Opposites Attract Conflict

YOU CAN ENCOURAGE CONFLICT in your story if you choose two lovers who have opposing characteristics. They'll tend to fall into opposition, making your job as a writer easier.

Look around you at the couples you know. You're certain to find a number of examples of the "opposites attract" theory. Now, look closer. Often, the very thing that attracted two people to each other is a trigger for conflict.

When two people form a bond of affection — whether it's friendship, parent-child, or life partner, they may have many things in common, but there will always be differences, ways in which they don't understand each other. They may speak two different languages, or come from cultures with extremely different customs. In a successful relationship, the bond can be enriched by both similarities and differences if the couple works towards understanding, working out compromises, and acceptance.

PRACTICING CONFLICT

WHAT PROBLEMS CAN YOU foresee for these couples?

- Bailey grew up an only child yearning for a big family. She falls in love with Kevin, who is one of seven siblings. She loves the family at first, until she's forced to deal with a host of unexpected problems. She's a deeply private person as a result of her solitary upbringing. Kevin is family oriented and believes telling their intimate secrets to his family isn't the same as "telling other people." When they get pregnant, Bailey tells Kevin she wants to keep the pregnancy a secret for a few weeks and he agrees. She's furious when he announces the pregnancy at the next family dinner, and Kevin can't understand why.

WRITING ROMANCE IN THE 21ST CENTURY: PLOTTING AND PLANNING

- Ella is an introverted woman who makes a habit of adopting stray dogs and children. She meets Glen, a brilliant, socially inept scientist and takes him under her motherly wing. He falls in love with her nurturing qualities but resents her "stray dog" motivation for caring about him.
- Ricardo, an emotionally repressed man who fears uncontrolled emotions. He falls passionately in love with Maria, a performer who exudes passion with every breath, but the depth of his own feelings for her terrifies him. (this is the premise of my book *Dance of Seduction*)
- Gerald is a minister in love with Eric, an openly gay member of his congregation. Gerald loves Eric and respects him for the obstacles he's overcome, but fears coming out about the relationship to his own family and his congregation.

SUMMARY: CONFLICT AND STRUGGLE
Goals + Obstacles = Conflict

WHENEVER A CHARACTER has a goal, conflict will result if another character opposes that goal. How hard the characters fight and how strong the conflict is will depend on how high the stakes are.

Factors affecting the degree of conflict:

- How much each character desires the goal.
- How confident each character is of achieving their goal.
- How flexible each character is about how and when the goal is achieved.
- How much each character will win or lose in the event of failure.
- The temperament of each character.

To create conflict in your novel ...

GIVE YOUR CHARACTER a goal with a high level of internal conflict, then have someone oppose that goal.

Being Nasty to Your Characters

A SATISFYING BOOK PITS characters against overwhelming odds, then leaves them to struggle through crisis after crisis until miraculously, victory is won. Your characters may win battles along the way. They may have a wonderful time on a date. They may laugh, make love, or even get married, but despite their victories, the problems keep coming until the reader, and sometimes even the writer, wonders if they'll survive.

The harder you make life for your characters, the better your readers will like the book. Until you reach the final scene, every scene should present new problems or new developments to old problems.

Forget everything you ever learned about being nice to people. To become a powerful storyteller, you must treat your characters terribly, dropping challenges to be overcome onto their path until the final victory is won.

9: Territory, the Bridge Between Character & Conflict

"The dog barking at you from behind his master's fence acts for a motive indistinguishable from that of his master when the fence was built." — Robert Ardrey, *The Territorial Imperative*.

PRIMITIVE URGES AND DANGER BUTTONS

ADAM AND EVE LIKE TO laugh together and sometimes they enjoy snuggling up under the bear fur, but first comes survival.

Every creature has a basic drive to seek shelter, a safe place to hide from predators, stockpile possessions or food, and ensure the survival of the species. Staking a claim to territory is a universal drive embedded deep in every species' brain, whether it's a bear occupying a cave in the woods, an eagle nesting high in a pine tree, a homeless person rolled into a blanket in an underground pedestrian tunnel, or a dog peeing on a tree trunk.

If our lovers are immersed in passion when a saber-toothed tiger slinks up behind them, they may not live long enough for Adam to impregnate Eve with an embryonic human baby. Adam and Eve need a safe place to procreate and nurture their offspring, where they can feel secure in a world full of danger. They need to establish territory and patrol the borders of that territory. They need to build a castle and surround it with a moat. A drawbridge. Locks on the doors. A guard dog. Territory.

Disputes over territory often get out of hand, causing stress and conflict.

Step back and take a look at the different kinds of territory your characters have, aspire to, or lay claim to. What do they value most? What territorial boundaries have they marked as their own?

Violation of territory can create powerful conflict, but even small territorial incursions can trigger primitive responses.

When the brain's security guard — the amygdala — sounds the alarm that territory has been invaded, it's responding to primitive wiring common to all living creatures. Although the security guard's ability to trigger adrenaline and strong emotions can save lives, it can be *way* out of proportion to the offense.

THE AMYGDALA HIJACK

*"The amygdala hijack is an **immediate, overwhelming emotional response** with a later realization that the response was inappropriately strong given the trigger. Daniel Goleman coined the term based on the work of neuroscientist Joseph LeDoux, which demonstrated that some emotional information travels directly from the thalamus to the amygdala without engaging the neocortex, or the higher brain regions. This causes a strong emotional response that precedes more rational thought."*
— gostrengths.com/what-is-an-amygdala-hijack[1]

TAKE A LOOK AT THE following headlines:

- *"Alec Baldwin appeared in court Monday where he was hit with two charges; the actor is accused of punching a New York driver during an alleged figh t over a parking space."* — ET Canada, 26 Nov 2018.

---

[1]. https://gostrengths.com/what-is-an-amygdala-hijack/

WRITING ROMANCE IN THE 21ST CENTURY: PLOTTING AND PLANNING

- *"Dog poo dispute in Spokane leads to arrest for felony assault."* — KXLYcom, 27 Feb 2019.
- *"Dog poo causes dispute between parishes and Swindon Burough Council."* — Swindon Advertiser, 30 Jan 2019.
- *"Woman rubs feces on neighbor's door in retaliation for dog pooping in yard."* — NBC12.com, 17 Sep 2018.

As irrational as dog poop disputes may seem, these fights of canine poop are not only common, they can also be tragic. The following is the sequence of a dispute I witnessed at a liveaboard marina in northern British Columbia. I won't embarrass the supposedly rational people who took part in the incident by naming any names.

THE GREAT DogSh*t WARS

- Sailor 1 finds doggie poo on the floats and, assuming he knows which dog deposited it, scoops it up and tosses it into Sailor 2's cockpit.
- Sailor 2 is furious when he discovers the deposit in his cockpit, scoops it up, and smears the excrement all over the front door of Sailor 1's pretty houseboat.
- Sailor 1 opens his door, sees the mess and flares out of control, pounding on the side of Sailor 2's boat and screaming, *"I'm going to kill you! I'm going to kill your Goddamned dog!"*
- Sailor 2 goes out for a weekend cruise, probably to get away from the dispute, and when he came back, Sailor 1 — who was also the marina manager — has moved another boat into Sailor 2's permanent berth, leaving Sailor 2 with nowhere to tie his boat up.

I DON'T KNOW WHAT THE ultimate result of the *Great DogSh*t Wars* was, but a few months later I learned of an incident at an Alaska marina where one sailor shot another over dog feces.

My parking space. My house. My territory. My safety. Every species has a subconscious security guard parked in the amygdala, ready to hijack the neocortex, preparing the animal, or the human, for battle.

"IT HAS BEEN SAID THAT man is a rational animal. All my life I have been searching for evidence which could support this." — Bertrand Russell

---

YOUR TERRITORY

"OWNERSHIP IS NOT LIMITED to material things. It can also apply to points of view. Once we take ownership of an idea — whether it's about politics or sports — what do we do? We love it perhaps more than we should. We prize it more than it is worth. And most frequently, we have trouble letting go of it because we can't stand the idea of its loss. What are we left with then? An ideology — rigid and unyielding." — Dan Ariely, *Predictably Irrational: The Hidden Forces That Shape Our Decisions*

IMAGINE YOU'RE AT A writers' conference. You walk into a room filled with strangers, scan the environment, and then go over to an empty chair. You place your pen, note pad, and cell phone on the table, then drape your jacket over the back of the chair. Sitting down, you make a friendly comment to the woman beside you and she responds with a smile.

WRITING ROMANCE IN THE 21ST CENTURY: PLOTTING AND PLANNING

When a man walks into the room and stands in front of the podium, the audience falls silent, waiting for him to speak. By standing at the front of the group, confidently waiting for silence, he has established leadership [territory].

"Good morning. I'd like to introduce our speaker, Jeanette Bestseller, author of the Covert Bay series of romances. Today, Jeanette will be presenting a workshop on *Building your Story World*."

He gestures and steps back, transferring the speaker's territory to Jeanette, who speaks for an hour, then suggests everyone take a 10-minute break to get refreshments.

You push back your chair, and head over to the refreshments table at the back of the room to get a cup of tea.

When you return, you find that someone has taken your seat.

"Excuse me," you say, "but that's my chair."

The invader makes no reply.

"There is an unspeakably primordial calculator, deep within you… it monitors exactly where you are positioned in society…" — Jordan Peterson

---

IF YOU WERE A RATIONAL being you might shrug and move your belongings to the empty chair on the other side of the aisle. But although your human brain's cerebral cortex is capable of rationality, the trigger for your territorial imperative is the primitive amygdala. The amygdala's function is to monitor the environment, always ready to detect threats and trigger an appropriate emotional response.

It doesn't matter that you do not *own* that chair, that losing custody of your place at the table has nothing to do with your survival. In the primitive part of your human brain, safety means keeping territory secure. *Secure territory means survival.*

Adrenaline pumps into your veins, flowing to your muscles, ramping up your heartbeat, driving the primitive *fight, freeze, or flight* urge. Your actual response depends on your temperament, your personality, your mood that day, the setting you are in, and past experiences.

You have a number of choices, among them are:

- Retreat, muttering audibly, "*The manners of some people.*"
- With stiff politeness, you say, "Excuse me. That's *my* chair," although you know the chair belongs to the hotel.
- Grab your possessions and stomp away.
- Grasp *your* chair and yank it out from under the usurper, who falls, sprawling, to the floor.
- Turn your back and sit down across the aisle, waiting for the usurper to leave before you collect your possessions.
- You take *Psychology Today*'s advice for what to do when faced with annoying people: "Take a deep breath, let it out slowly and focus on breathing comfortably."

The security guard in your hindbrain wants you to do something definite, but if you retreat, sit down across the aisle and wait until the workshop is dismissed to collect your jacket, note pad, and phone, that adrenaline will grumble in your veins, a pressure urging you to act. You'll feel the tension and know you've just moved down a degree or two in the hierarchy.

It was my chair!

Territorial disputes are at the heart of most human conflict. Tracy shoots Bob in a dispute over a parking space. An exhausted mother screams at her child in an argument over a messy room. Two live-aboard sailors fight with each other over dog poop. One pulls out a gun.

Irrational? Out of proportion? Yes. Human? Absolutely.

WRITING ROMANCE IN THE 21ST CENTURY: PLOTTING AND PLANNING

My parking space. My house. My idea. My territory. My safety. Deep in the limbic system of every primate's brain, the amygdala is constantly scanning the environment, monitoring and interpreting incoming data, ready to sound the alarm at the first sign of territorial threat.

UNDERSTANDING THE STRESS RESPONSE

"WHEN SOMEONE CONFRONTS an oncoming car or other danger, the eyes or ears (or both) send the information to the amygdala, an area of the brain that contributes to emotional processing. The amygdala interprets the images and sounds. When it perceives danger, it instantly sends a distress signal to the hypothalamus. This area of the brain functions like a command center, communicating with the rest of the body through the nervous system so that the person has the energy to fight or flee." — Understanding the Stress Response, Harvard Health Publishing

DEFINING CHARACTERS' TERRITORY

WHEN YOU'RE PLANNING, plotting, and writing, be on the lookout for potential areas of territorial conflict. Whether it's physical territory, financial territory, social territory, intellectual territory or emotional territory, the amygdala of all primates is perpetually on guard against trespassers crossing territorial boundaries.

When your characters territorial boundaries are threatened, they'll react in one of two ways — fight or flight. There is a third option, to freeze, which is also a way of fleeing, retreating inside your own mind.

TERRITORIAL PLOT DEVELOPMENT

VANESSA GRANT

A FEW YEARS AGO, AT a writers' brainstorming session I shared an idea for a romance involving Ricardo, an Ecuadorian-Canadian archaeologist who had been a good friend of the female protagonist in *Catalina's Lover*.

The brainstorming session had come at a good time because I'd fallen for Ricardo while I was writing *Catalina and* was in the planning stages of his love story.

I arrived at this writers' gathering, my mind filled with Ricardo and the lover I was creating for him. I have no idea *why* I picked a Canadian doctor with a limp as the perfect match for my archeologist — something about opposites attract, perhaps.

I'd put a lot of work into crafting this heroine, but when I began talking about my story concept, all that time I'd spent creating a lover for Ricardo went *whooshing* down the drain. I could hear my own words settle into the carpet as the room fell silent.

Remembering that moment, the phrase *flogging a dead horse* comes to mind. I'd been working so hard, so seriously, to create the perfect lover for Ricardo that I'd lost sight of the fun. My planning was so intense that I'd ignored chemistry, conflict, and romance.

As for territory, no matter how many words I threw out into the room, casting about for territorial conflict, no one in the room could dream up even a whiff of trouble between the two of them. Ricardo was serious, studious, dedicated to his career — but he was also sexy, intuitive, and mysterious. But although the woman I'd constructed for him would be a good candidate for a friend, there wasn't a breath of fire or passion.

No wonder I hadn't been able to settle on a name for her.

Someone in the group suggested deleting my nameless limping doctor and giving Ricardo a different love partner.

Yes. Absolutely. Good idea!

The moment I decided to dump this nameless woman, my muse woke up.

WRITING ROMANCE IN THE 21ST CENTURY: PLOTTING AND PLANNING

I understood Ricardo Swan's self-concept from *Catalina's Lover*. He prided himself on being rational and cool, the detachment resulting from a childhood navigating the explosive territory between his rational father and his fiery Latin mother. His personal history gave him an aversion to being possessed emotionally by any woman. Even his love for archaeology was tempered by cool reason.

Hmm. Cool reason, but Ricardo has to fall in love, and love doesn't blossom from the brain's cerebral cortex. But Ricardo must have strong emotion in there somewhere, repressed by a childhood spent on the razor's edge of his parents' explosive battleground.

His public face might be cool reason, but there must be a fire burning behind those walls he'd built around his public persona. Ice and fire were both part of his psychological territory.

He needed a lover who would challenge his self-concept. Limping Doctor wouldn't do. They might be lifelong friends, but they made dismally dull lovers.

Hmm. A lover to burn through Ricardo's boundaries. His cool, rational public image might be built of stone, but inside those walls was a cave, and at the heart of the cave was fire. Ricardo needed a woman who challenged those walls. A sensual Latin woman to burn through his icy walls, creating an internal battle between his rational self-concept and his hidden emotional passion.

Ricardo needed Maria. A performer, a singer and flamenco dancer. A woman in conflict with her own nature.

Suddenly, I knew exactly what my story needed to flash into life. Where Ricardo was cool outside, denying his inner passion, Maria's passion lived onstage, a sensual Latin singer and dancer, the walls around her passionate fire were the boundaries of the stage itself.

Offstage, she was a different woman, willingly sequestered by her family. Her motivation for this internal denial of her own passionate nature was a prime motivating event. As a sheltered teenager, she was raped by a teacher she had a crush on. Now, as a woman, she funnels all her passion into her singing and dancing, building a wall between her outer fire and the frozen emptiness in her heart.

The stage is her territory, and she guards it well.

In that brainstorming session, Ricardo and Maria came vibrantly to life. The strong internal conflict between the lovers and their incompatible territories immediately drove them into external conflict, and *Dance of Seduction* virtually wrote itself.

When Ricardo first saw Maria onstage, his inner fire flared and he was a goner. When the security guard in Maria's amygdala sounded yellow alert, she used every defense she'd built around her heart, but they all failed — because this time Maria undermined her own defenses. By the time her amygdala realized the danger and sounded a red alert, it was too late to reinforce her borders. She'd already fallen in love with Ricardo.

The moment these two characters broached each other's personal territory, conflict became inevitable and the story almost wrote itself. In the end, the two characters re-drew their territorial boundaries to make new territory encompassing both.

TERRITORIAL CONFLICT IN THE MOVIES

TWO PEOPLE WITH INCOMPATIBLE territory will always experience conflict. For every character you can make up, there's another who will violate that character's territory.

The next time you're reading a book or watching a movie, be on the lookout for the role of territory in creating conflict.

He's a man who wants to save the rain forest. She wants to help him. For this to make a story, the characters need conflict. He's a man who's determined to save the rain forest his own way, a man who won't play

WRITING ROMANCE IN THE 21ST CENTURY: PLOTTING AND PLANNING

by the rules. She's a woman who believes in the rules; she even makes some of them. The 1992 movie *Medicine Man* is driven by this basic conflict between character territories.

Patricia Briggs' *Mercy Thompson* series of urban fantasy novels is a masterpiece of character-driven territorial conflict. Mercy, a Volkswagen mechanic, is a coyote shapeshifter who grew up in a werewolf pack. Not surprisingly, she's had it with being bossed around by werewolves. Her neighbor Adam is Alpha of the Columbia Basin werewolf pack, and as bossy as you would expect a werewolf alpha to be. Mercy fights back in her own way, including deliberately parking one of her oldest VW's in plain sight of Adam's front porch. The series, which follows Mercy and Adam's love relationship and offers a rich selection of good characters, is a must-read for anyone interested in a guide to territorial conflict and top-quality world-building.

SUMMARY: DEVELOPING TERRITORIAL CONFLICT

- Develop character self-concepts and motivations, then...
- Define the areas of territory that each primary character must patrol to maintain their self-concept.
- Determine the most feared dangers from your character's point of view. Remember that the strongest red alert dangers may stem from prime motivating events in the character's past.
- Determine how your character dealt with territorial invasions in the past. When amygdala pushes the alarm button, adrenaline will push your character to make a *fight or flight* decision based on past behavior.
- Conflict between lovers should have a focus. They need real conflict, real problems. Ask yourself whether there is a natural conflict between any of the physical, emotional, and

psychological territories of either lover.
- If your characters' territorial boundaries don't reveal an inherent conflict, you may have trouble developing an interesting plot. Look deeper. Look again. Or, as I did in *The Dance of Seduction*, recast your story. Try tossing out the lover you feel less committed to and creating a new one.
- Examine how the territorial habits of your lovers will affect each other as their territories cross. This is the essence of the conflict driving your plot. This is where problems develop for your lovers, and where they stop being rational.
- Completely rational characters do not make for exciting reading. Humans have the capacity for cool reason, but behavioral science has demonstrated that our human brains are predictably irrational in certain situations. Check out Dan Ariely's books: *Predictably Irrational* and *The (Honest) Truth about Dishonesty*, or search for Dan Ariely on YouTube. You'll discover a universe of exciting story ideas solidly based on science.

"We usually think of ourselves as sitting in the driver's seat, with ultimate control over the decisions we made and the direction our life takes; but, alas, this perception has more to do with our desires — with how we want to view ourselves — than with reality." — Dan Ariely, *Predictably Irrational*.

10: The Power of Setting

"CHOSEN CAREFULLY, THE right setting can help characterize the story's cast, deliver backstory in a way that enriches, convey emotion, supply tension, and accomplish a host of other things to give readers a one-of-a-kind experience. In fact, out of all the ingredients that make a compelling story, setting is one of the most versatile yet often underutilized.
— Angela Ackerman and Becca Puglisi, *The Urban Setting Thesaurus: A Writer's Guide to City Spaces*

LOVERS SELDOM FALL in love in a vacuum. They move through time, surrounded by families, coworkers, pets, and possessions. They live their lives in homes, offices, cities, towns, hospitals, farms, cruise ships, space stations, lighthouses, submarines, oil rigs — in an endless universe of fascinating settings.

Browse through the romance section in your bookstore. On a typical day you'll might find a variety of settings: Scotland in the 17th Century, the present-day Seattle waterfront, the Toronto financial district, and a scattering that could include a Nova Scotia village, a Wyoming ranch, a mountain village in Peru, and a Martian desert.

As humans, we occupy space. The characteristics of that space influence our lives. If you conceive of your setting as separate character in your story, you can use the opportunities and restrictions of your story's environment to draw your reader deeply into your imaginary world.

You are a storyteller, creator of the universe your lovers occupy. As creator, you are free to place your characters in any setting you choose, free to manipulate the weather, the sunsets, the earthquakes, tidal waves, landslides and global disasters. You control the beauty of the star-studded sky, the seductiveness of the ocean waves whispering under the northern lights.

Use your freedom well. Choose the features of your story world carefully, breathing life into you're your characters' world.

WHAT YOU NEED TO KNOW ABOUT YOUR SETTING
Atmosphere
THE ATMOSPHERE OR MOOD of your setting can evoke an emotional response in the reader, preparing them for coming events.

What mood might your setting stir? Gay and festive like a Mexican city at carnival? Saturated with history and tragedy like a Greek ruin? Is the beach your character stands on peaceful with the soft hiss of white surf whispering across the sand, or crowded and chaotic, filled with the laughter of children playing?

Does your crowded Mexican marketplace feel open and friendly, joyous with the sound of mariachi music? Or do you hear the murmur of quiet voices and the rustle of merchants packing up their fruit stands for the day?

How isolated is your chosen location from the rest of the world? Can a snow slide cut off the population from the outside world, or can you catch a jet to anywhere at the local airport?

What are the sights, the smells, the sounds, and the touches? You'll want to evoke the flavor of your setting for your readers, and to do so you'll need to understand it yourself.

Impact on Characters
How does your chosen location affect the local people? How will it affect your characters? Your setting may be merely a backdrop for your story, or it could be filled with sensory, evocative detail. Some settings create a crucible that exerts pressure against the characters, challenging their very lives.

WRITING ROMANCE IN THE 21ST CENTURY: PLOTTING AND PLANNING

Here are a few examples of the varying impact of settings from my own books:

- In *Awakening Dreams,* I wrote about a female tax auditor and a male pilot who crashed in the remote wilderness of northern coastal British Columbia. The wilderness setting provided many of my characters' problems: the cold north Pacific seawater that caries warmth away from the body 25 times faster than air of the same temperature, sucking heat from the body's core; the dense undergrowth they had to hike through to find rescue; and the local wildlife. This setting was remote and life threatening, an essential part of the story.
- In *Angela's Affair,* I wrote about a female canvas worker in Port Townsend, Washington, and a wealthy businessman from Canada. The picturesque shipbuilding town provided local color, but the novel could have been set in any North American Pacific coastal town without much change to the plot.
- In *Catalina's Lover,* I wrote the story of an American archaeologist and a Peruvian landowner. Because their cultural differences were one of the biggest problems they had to overcome, the Peruvian setting was crucial of the story. This book could not have been set anywhere else than the South American mountains without a complete rewrite.
- *If You Loved Me* was originally written as the story of a Canadian surgeon desperate to find her son, who was overdue returning from a kayaking trip on British Columbia's remote north coast. Because the story's nontraditional plot elements didn't work for my Mills & Boon editor in England, I decided to submit to Zebra Books, who were then looking for American stories. Although the Canadian coastal wilderness setting was crucial to this romance, I decided that

Emma's medical practice didn't need to be located in Canada. So, I shifted her job to an American hospital in Seattle, kept the Canadian wilderness — which was the main part of the book — for the search and rescue, and sold the book to Zebra.

After writing over three dozen novels, I've come to the realization it's easier to write a book with a strong setting, one that affects the lives of the people in my story. I've also noticed that my readers often tell me their favorites are the books in which setting has played a crucial role.

If your characters have strong feelings about the setting, those feelings will give the reader the sensation of being there. If you set your romance in a small town, ask yourself how the characters feel about the town they live in.

- Is it the only home Country Girl has ever had?
- Does Country Girl's love partner, City Boy, find the small-town pace irritating?
- Will these feelings intensify during the course of the story, or will City Boy fall in love with both Country Girl and the world she lives in?

Exotic Settings

Wherever you set your novel, the location is likely to be fresh and exotic to someone, somewhere. Ask yourself what makes your setting unique. What's the one thing you would want to show your readers? People from far away will find it exotic, and the locals will read it and feel at home.

Playing it Safe

If you set your story in a location you've visited but have never lived in, play it safe by making your protagonist a stranger to the location.

WRITING ROMANCE IN THE 21ST CENTURY: PLOTTING AND PLANNING

Although I lived in Mexico for two years and have set several books there, I've never lived in a Mexican household and I know there are ways in which I don't think like a Mexican national.

When I began writing *Dance of Seduction*, I needed my heroine to be a Mexican singer, but I was nervous about writing a character whose culture I had only observed from the outside. To play it safe, I decided to give Maria a two-year period during which she'd been sent to Los Angeles for her high school education. Similarly, when I wrote *Catalina's Lover*, I had my Peruvian hero educated in England and the United States, giving him an additional seven years living and working outside Peru, thereby explaining any non-Latin speech or behavior.

SOUNDS, SIGHTS, SMELLS, touches and tastes are capable of stirring emotions and memories in the human brain. The most powerful of these is smell, which is the most closely connected to the hippocampus (the part of our brain responsible for our memories) and our friend the limbic system (which regulates our emotions).

For this reason, the use of sensory words can evoke strong images and emotions in the minds of your readers.

WRITING ABOUT SETTING

Cynthia Dyson-Paige was still rehearsing what she would say to Jonathan Halley. She'd been practicing the words for hours. "I thought you'd want to help Allan. He needs help ... "

AS YOU READ THE ABOVE passage, you probably assumed Cynthia to be a woman, but is she indoors? Outdoors? On a beach? In a restaurant? Or in a vacuum?

Unless the author provides enough information to evoke a sense of place, the reader will be floating around in the middle of nowhere. As the storyteller, it's your job to make it easy for the readers to form a mental picture based on your words.

Here's that opening passage as I wrote it in my book, *On Johnny's Terms* (This book was previously titled *The Moon Lady's Lover*)

When the jet landed in Vancouver, Cynthia Dyson-Paige was still rehearsing what she would say to Jonathan Halley. She'd been practicing the words all through the four-hour flight from Toronto.

She rented a car at the airport, wincing as her credit card went through the point of sale machine. Then she crawled into Vancouver with the morning rush-hour traffic, still rehearsing the encounter to come.

"I thought you'd want to help Allan. He needs help ... "

With the added details I've given above, the reader knows Cynthia just disembarked from a cross-Canada jet airplane flight and that she's short of money.

My objective was to give the reader just enough information to visualize Cynthia and her surroundings. I can assume most readers are familiar with jets, credit cards, and rush-hour traffic, either from their own experience or from movies or other books, so I didn't need to waste words describing these things. I also dropped in a couple of details designed to trigger both speculation and curiosity in the reader's mind.

When I wrote *With Strings Attached,* I began my protagonist Molly's arrival at Gabriola Island. Because few of my readers would be familiar with the complex details of travel from the British Columbia coast to the Gulf Islands nestled against Vancouver Island, I scattered travel details into Molly's inner thoughts. Here's the passage.

Molly swung the steering wheel to the left and followed a green car through a controlled intersection. Had she just turned on to the Trans-Canada highway? These British Columbians had a nerve, calling it the Trans-Canada highway after interrupting it for a ferry crossing of

WRITING ROMANCE IN THE 21ST CENTURY: PLOTTING AND PLANNING

Georgia Strait. Where the devil were the signs? Could you turn off Route One to that other ferry? Or — Gabriola Island. It must be an Indian name. Or was it Spanish? Gabriola. Yes, Spanish. She knew so little about it. A gulf island nestled against Vancouver Island...

FICTIONAL SETTINGS

"One way to make your writing seem authentic is to write about the things you know. Sometimes, though, plots may suggest themselves which cannot be situated in your home town or peopled with your friends or neighbors. When this is the case, you create the illusion of reality through a combination of research and verbal sleight-of-hand." — Lawrence Block, Telling Lies for Fun & Profit.

MOST OF MY WISDOM ABOUT writing fictional settings comes from Chapter 41 of Lawrence Block's wonderful book, *Telling Lies for Fun & Profit*. Chapter 41 is titled, *"Hum a few Bars... and Fake It."*

Most of my novels are set in places I've either visited or lived in, but sometimes I've had to make it up, or as Lawrence Block would say, "Hum a few bars and fake it."

Some years ago I published a dark thriller called *September 7th* under the pen name Val Cameron. The plot centered around the activities of a generational Satanic cult. I did masses of research on Satanic Ritual Abuse for the story, but when it came to the small California town where the cult's leaders were living, I wasn't about to point my finger at a map and say, "Here's where those evil Satanists live!"

The events that took place at the San Diego Airport or in an unnamed Marina weren't going to cause me any trouble, but when my sleuths were sneaking about at night in a small town, I needed to know my way about well enough not to stumble over my own tracks because I couldn't visualize the geography.

I solved the problem by giving a real California coastal town of appropriate size a fake name, then changing the street names on the map for the areas of town where my sleuths were going to be prowling. I added an X to the location that marked the home of the cult's matriarch so I wouldn't get mixed up.

The altered map made the job of describing the sleuths' nighttime prowling realistically enough for the reader to form a picture of the terrain and the houses, without putting the label of "Satanic cult" onto an existing California town.

My general policy on real vs. imagined settings is to use fictional settings if naming a real locale might reflect badly on any living people or existing businesses. With the exception of acknowledgments, dedications, and a couple of occasions involving charity auctions where people bid for the right to have their name used for a character in one of my books, I don't name real people in my books.

If I'm writing about a place I've never been — such as Peru, the setting of *Catalina's Lover* — I do masses of research. Without the help of the Nanaimo Public library, Ronald Wright's *Cut Stones and Crossroads,* and Elizabeth Devine and Nancy L. Braganti's *The Travelers' Guide to Latin American Customs and Manners* both of which I located at Vancouver's *World Book and Map Company,* I would never have been able to deliver the South American romance my Mills & Boon editor kept urging me to write. Sadly, the fascinating *World Book and Map Company* has since disappeared from Vancouver's Granville Street.

WRITING ROMANCE IN THE 21ST CENTURY: PLOTTING AND PLANNING

I used to do most of my research at the library and in bookstores until the 21st Century brought me the vast resources of online search engines.

SUMMARY: GUIDELINES FOR SETTING

- When you're developing your book, make a note of things about the setting that interest you and plan to weave them into your story.
- In describing setting, the emotions evoked may be more important than the physical details. A stormy day can be used to foreshadow an emotional storm in the characters. A sunny day may contrast with the violence of a terrible argument.
- Determine what your chosen setting feels like to locals and strangers.
- Define the impact of your setting on your characters. Will isolation affect your story? Will cultural characteristics contribute to your conflict?
- Is your setting merely a background for your story, or is it an essential factor? The answer will determine how much space you give to describing the impact of setting on your characters. The more power setting has over your characters, the more memorable your readers will find it.
- How do your characters feel about the setting? Strong feelings and powerful memories about the setting will make it seem more real.
- If you're writing about a setting you don't know intimately, play it safe by making your viewpoint character a stranger to the setting.
- Determine what makes your setting exotic to outsiders and include those details in your description.

- Make a note of the setting elements that interest you. These same elements may also interest the reader.
- If you're creating fictional settings, make them realistic. If, like me, you don't have a highly visual memory, check your research sources against your memory to avoid making mistakes.
- There's no reason not to use the real name of a business, unless you plan to have negative events occur on the premises or say negative things about the owners or employees. If you're going to have a character poisoned in a restaurant, make it a fake restaurant.
- Include sensory data — sights, sounds, touches, smells and tastes in your descriptions. This will stimulate the imagination of your readers, drawing them into your story world.
- Provide your reader with enough information to form a mental picture of each scene.

11: Scene & Sequel — the Skin and Bones of Story

YOU KNOW YOUR CHARACTERS' hopes, dreams, and fears. You understand the conflict that will drive your story. You know where you'll set your book and how that location will affect your characters' destiny. What else do you need before you put your notes aside and start writing?

PLOTTER or PANTSTER?

SOME WRITERS KNOW EVERY detail before they start writing Chapter One. Their characters seldom surprise them. Because they've created a detailed outline of their plot and fully developed their characters before writing the book, they're known as *Plotters*.

John Grisham says ...

"I don't start a novel until I have lived with the story for awhile to the point of actually writing an outline and after a number of books I've learned that the more time I spend on the outline the easier the book is to write. And if I cheat on the outline I get in trouble with the book."

Other authors begin writing without knowing where the story will wander and what secrets lie hidden beneath the surface of their characters. These writers are known as *Pansters* because they write "by the seat of their pants." Their characters' actions are a constant surprise, the events unfolding with each page the Panster writes.

Margaret Attwood says ...

"When I'm writing a novel, what comes first is an image, scene, or voice. Something fairly small. Sometimes that seed is contained in a poem I've already written. The structure or design gets worked out in the course of the writing. I couldn't write the other way round, with structure first. It would be too much like paint-by-numbers."

And Stephen King says ...

"Outlines are the last resource of bad fiction writers who wish to God they were writing masters' theses."

Most of us fall somewhere between these two extremes. Over the years I've experimented with a variety of ways to nurse a story idea from the original spark to final scene. Every book is different for me, but in general I'm most comfortable starting somewhere in the middle. If one technique doesn't work, I'll shift to another, but generally before I dive into a story, I want to know my protagonist at the deepest level. I want to know the prime motivating events (PMEs) and prime motivating forces (PMFs) that drive the major characters, the obstacles they'll face, and the character growth they'll experience before *The End*. If I've done this groundwork well, my characters will be nudging me awake in the morning, teasing me with scraps of the future they visualize for themselves.

Like sulky teenagers, my characters don't like to be pushed around. The odd time I've tried writing a detailed plot outline ahead of time, I've felt trapped by it and often miss the signals my characters are giving me, only to land up stalled further along in the story.

SCENE and SEQUEL

FOLLOWING THE WAY IN which we live our lives in pursuit of goals as humans, the building blocks of scene and sequel provide a logical, yet flexible storytelling structure that works for both Plotters and Pansters.

WRITING ROMANCE IN THE 21ST CENTURY: PLOTTING AND PLANNING

- *Scenes* engage the reader by creating drama, moving the story forward with conflict, action, and dialog. The action of a scene is *external*, visible to others.
- *Sequels* clarify the meaning of scenes that went before, summarize the events between scenes, giving characters new goals to move forward with.

In *Techniques of the Selling Writer*, Dwight Swain defines a scene as "a unit of conflict lived through by character and reader" and a sequel as, "a unit of transition that links two scenes."

Decades later, Swain's student Jack Bickham listed four characteristics of a real-life scene in his book, *Writing and Selling Your Novel*.

Bickham describes a scene as ...

"... *a component of the story which plays out in the story now, from a single viewpoint, told moment-by-moment, with no summary — and what the characters do has ... downstream effects, impact on later developments which determine the course of the rest of the story. — Jack M. Bickham, Writing and Selling Your Novel*

LIVING IN PURSUIT OF GOALS

AS HUMANS, WE LIVE our lives in pursuit of goals, following the same pattern of scene and sequel that Dwight Swain and Jack M. Bickham recommend to writers.

- We form short-term and long-term *goals*.
- We are *motivated* to take action toward our goals.
- When we take action, we often experience opposition.
- When we fight that opposition, we sometimes lose.
- Even when we *win*, the victory frequently comes with a price.
- After each battle, we experience a variety of *emotions*.

- We *review* what happened, experience the *dilemma* of trying to figure out what to do next, and finally form a new *goal*.
- When we put our new goal into *action*, the cycle begins again.

We may win a battle, only to find that there's another obstacle ahead. We fight another battle, and another ... and if we're persistent and perhaps lucky, we finally win our goal. Victory!

This is the story of human life: goals, conflict and struggle, wins and losses, disasters, regrouping and rising again to fight the next battle.

When you write good fiction that follows our life patterns as humans, you enable your readers to suspend disbelief and step into the world of story. That's what you want, and it's what your reader wants.

Scene and Sequel is a model of storytelling that gives writers clarity, simplicity, and flexibility.

THE STRUCTURE OF SCENE AND SEQUEL

"The scene ... has conflict at its heart, but is not static. It is a dynamic structural component with a definite internal pattern which forces the story to move forward as the scene plays — and as a result of its ending."
— Jack M. Bickham, Scene and Structure

Scene Structure

- *GOAL* - Every character should enter a scene with their own agenda, an immediate, specific scene goal, which should be clearly disclosed to the reader. This will prompt the reader to form a scene question which can be answered with a yes or no; for example, *Will Jose win the race?*
- *CONFLICT* - conflict is introduced and developed.

Someone opposes the character's scene goal. To keep readers turning pages, the scene conflict must move the story forward.
- *DISASTER* - the character's failure to reach the goal is a tactical disaster, which has downstream effects on the next scene.

THE DISASTER PORTION of the scene answers the question: *Does the focal character achieve the goal?*
There are three possible answers:

- No
- No, and furthermore — !
- Yes, *but* there's a catch

Note that until the end of the story when all the loose ends are tied up, it's important for the focal character to exit the scene with a problem, the disaster that gives the reader something to worry about. If all issues were resolved at the end of the scene, there would be nothing left to maintain suspense.

"[The disaster ...] must raise an intriguing question for the future — a question designed to keep your reader reading. To that end, no better device has ever been conceived than the confrontation of your focal character with disaster." — Dwight V. Swain, Techniques of the Selling Writer

༶

THE MOMENT THE SCENE ends, struck by an unanticipated but logical *disaster*, your viewpoint character reacts. This reaction is the *sequel*.

Sequel Structure

- *EMOTION* - your viewpoint character experiences an emotional reaction to the disaster
- *DILEMMA / QUANDARY* - and begins to contemplate the new situation, uncertain what to do next
- *DECISION* - finally coming to a new, goal-oriented decision
- *ACTION* - which results in your character taking action toward a new goal.

The action at the end of the sequel moves the story forward into the next scene. The wise author will keep the reader wondering about the outcome until the final, satisfying scene.

Let's look at a simple example of scene and sequel.

ALIX AND THE DEBATE
The Scene ...

- *GOAL*: Our viewpoint character Alix has entered a debate. Her goal is to win the prize money to pay her university fees.
- *CONFLICT:* The debate begins. Alix's three opponents also want to win, but Mac is the only one Alix is worried about. During the debate, the exchange between Alix and Mac becomes heated.
- *DISASTER*: *No, and furthermore...* Alix loses the debate to Mac, *and furthermore* she discovers that Mac, whom she called "an idiot" in the debate, is the new manager at the restaurant where she works part time. If she loses her job, she won't be able to pay her university fees and she may have to drop out of university.

WRITING ROMANCE IN THE 21ST CENTURY: PLOTTING AND PLANNING

The Sequel ...

DISASTER MOVES ALIX into the Sequel, where she experiences...

- *EMOTION*: Alix is furious with Mac for winning, and with herself for letting him win. Underlying her anger is disappointment and worry about how to pay her university fees.
- The DILEMMA: Emotions exhausted, she ponders her financial dilemma, reviewing her options. Her mother has no money to spare, and she hates the thought of approaching her estranged father.
- DECISION: Finally, she decides her only option is to apologize to Mac for calling him an idiot and beg him for more shifts at her part time job. Alix must overcome her pride and face Mac at work.
- ACTION: Alix makes an appointment to meet with Mac at her workplace, which sets up the next scene.

Note that the character's decision at the end of the sequel leads directly into a future scene. With each scene and sequel leading into the next, the reader keeps turning pages to discover what happens next.

INSIDE THE SCENE

WHETHER YOU'RE A PLOTTER or a Panster, when it comes to writing the individual scenes, the best advice I've ever read comes from Jack M. Bickham's *Writing and Selling Your Novel*.

When talking about the nuts and bolts of writing, Bickham reminds us that most human actions take place in response to some event or action, and that *stimulus* and *response* transactions are the driving force of our stories.

Whether you're planning, plotting, writing or revising your story, think of playing ping pong and focus each scene on *following the ball*.

When two characters cohabit a scene, Character A's action or spoken word becomes the stimulus for Character B's response, which then becomes the stimulus for A's next response. These transactions weave together, building a chain of cause and effect for the reader to follow.

The lovers in my novel *When Love Returns* haven't seen each other in years. When Julie, newly returned to Gabriola Island, backs her car into the path of David's dump truck, he rushes to her car, panicked, and discovers Julie at the wheel.

- *Action:* Julie backs her car into David's dump truck, providing ...
- *Stimulus for David*, who leaps out of his truck, discovers Julie is alive, but in unknown condition. He's frightened, but relieved that she is conscious.
- *David's verbal Response*: "Can you move? Does it hurt to breathe?"
- *Stimulus for Julie*: Shock of crash, David's appearance, and question.
- *Julie's Response*: Silence. Internally, she's nauseous, feels guilty because the accident was her fault.
- *Stimulus for David*: Julie appears unharmed, but his fear and panic produce adrenaline that now transforms to anger in his relief.
- *David's Response*: "I could have killed you. I damned near did. One day you'll kill yourself with your nonsense!"
- *Stimulus for Julie*: David shouting at her.
- *Julie's Response*: (Defensive) "I didn't stop to think — " *provides stimulus for David.*

WRITING ROMANCE IN THE 21ST CENTURY: PLOTTING AND PLANNING

- *David's Response*: "Damn it, Julie! Do you ever think?"

WITH STIMULUS, RESPONSE, and adrenaline pounding in both Julie and David's bloodstreams, they've moved from a collision of vehicles into an argument that brings up old frustrations from the past.

You know your characters. You know their goals, dreams, and fears. Whether you're a panster, a plotter, or somewhere in between, you'll need to know the story goal before you finish your story. In your romantic novel, the story goal is probably something like, "David and Julie overcome their difficulties and achieve a loving partnership."

You'll also need a mental picture of how your story starts, for example, *Julie backs down the drive into the path of David's dump truck*. Starting from that point, you can make your way through a series of stimulus and response transactions until you get to the end of the story.

Whether you're planning, plotting, or somewhere in between, when something happens in your book, ask yourself how your character would react to that stimulus.

What will Julie do when David accuses her of recklessness?

Because I already know Julie, I know she'll remember the times David bossed her around when she was a kid, the childish moment when she was twelve and asked the adult David to marry her, and her humiliation at his reaction. Because she knows the accident is her fault, she's bound to be both humiliated and defensive. Then, if he keeps up the attack, she'll become angry.

Is it realistic for David to shout at Julie moments after hitting her with his truck?

I certainly think so. He's shaken from the accident, can't get rid of the horror of that moment when he thought he'd killed her. At the whiplash end of relief, the primitive *fight or flight* surge of adrenaline is still raging through his veins and his brain, hijacking his rational cerebral cortex.

Whenever your character speaks or acts, ask yourself if there was an appropriate stimulus for the character's action. If the answer is *no*, your reader won't be able to make sense of your character's behavior either.

If David had shouted, "Damn it, Julie! Do you ever think?" without the provocation of the accident, readers would be justifiably confused. Confused readers are likely to lose interest in characters who don't make sense.

Pick up your favorite novel and begin rereading it. Stop at each action and see if you can find a stimulus for that action. That stimulus could come from the character's own thoughts, from the actions of other characters, or from external events.

You'll probably discover that your favorite novel is one long chain of stimulus-response transactions, assembled into a string of scenes and sequels.

SUMMARY: SCENE AND SEQUEL

SCENE AND SEQUEL PROVIDES a logical, yet flexible storytelling structure that drives the story towards the ending with a pattern of scenes containing conflict, action, and dialogue; and sequels in which characters review and clarify the meaning of scenes that went before, and form new goals to move forward with.

The scene has 3 elements: GOAL, CONFLICT, DISASTER.

- GOAL: The viewpoint character enters with a scene goal, an agenda which can be stated in the form of a question.
- CONFLICT: The character struggles to achieve the goal but is opposed by an adversary or adversaries. This conflict manifests itself in a series of STIMULUS and RESPONSE transactions which could be subtle or direct, verbal or physical.
- DISASTER: There are three types of disaster, any one of

which will necessitate the viewpoint character having to find new ways to move forward toward the ultimate goal. Type 1: the goal is not achieved. Type 2: Not only does your character fail to achieve the goal, furthermore, there's another problem. Type 3. Although the goal is achieved, there's a catch, creating another obstacle between your viewpoint character and the desired goal.

The Sequel, which follows a scene or scenes, has four elements:

- EMOTION: Your viewpoint character experiences emotion in reaction to the previous scene or scenes.
- DILEMMA/QUANDARY: The character contemplates this new dilemma, uncertain what to do next.
- DECISION: The character solves the quandary and comes to a new, goal-oriented decision.
- ACTION: Having made a decision, the viewpoint character takes the first step toward the new goal.

This pattern of scenes and sequels continues until the end of the story, when the heroic protagonist achieves the story goal.

12: The Hero's Journey — the Heart and Soul of Story

IN *The Writer's Journey: Mythic Structure for Writers,* author Christopher Vogler writes ...

"The Hero's Journey is a pattern that seems to extend in many dimensions, describing more than one reality. It accurately describes, among other things, the process of making a journey, the necessary working parts of a story, the joys and despairs of being a writer, and the passage of a soul through life ... The pattern of the hero's journey is universal, appearing in every culture, in every time."

IN 1949, COMPARATIVE mythologist Joseph Campbell published *The Hero with a Thousand Faces.* This transformational book defined the functions and pattern of a universal underlying structure shared by the enduring myths and stories he found from around the world. He called this mythic structure *The Hero's Journey.*

Forty-three years later, Hollywood story consultant Christopher Vogler published *The Writer's Journey: Mythic Structure for Writers,* a deep exploration of Joseph Campbell's work adapted for modern writers and storytellers. The book quickly rose to the best seller list, becoming one of the most popular books on writing and garnering glowing reviews from authors, screenwriters, and film producers and directors.

The Writer's Journey became my constant companion for months after I purchased the book. I would read a few paragraphs each day, then muse on the theories, the ideas, and how they resonated with me.

WRITING ROMANCE IN THE 21ST CENTURY: PLOTTING AND PLANNING

I spotted the hero's journey and its archetypes wherever I looked: in every person I met, every story I read, every movie I watched, and in my own life.

Inevitably, the concept, the stages, and the archetypes of the hero's journey became a part of my life, of my writing, and my storytelling, and it wasn't long before I began teaching the hero's journey in my own workshops and writing courses.

The thing I love most about the hero's journey as that it is NOT a formula, but an exploration of the life journeys we travel as human beings. Our minds travel this journey in dreams, in fantasy, and in our lives. The hero's journey describes a natural pattern of storytelling that Joseph Campbell discovered exists in all cultures, during all times. The hero's journey is the path we as humans use to explore and manifest meaning in our dreams and our lives.

There is an underlying, universal pattern to the mythology in every culture, in every time.

It goes like this ...

In the early part of the story, the protagonist receives a call to adventure, just as we ourselves receive calls to adventure.

The call to adventure creates a turning point in our lives, and in the lives of our characters. We must make a choice; whether to accept the call and its associated risks, or to refuse, turning our back on adventure. We, and our characters, might resist the call. After all, change is risky and the hazards we will encounter on the path ahead are unknown.

Ultimately, if there is to be a story, if we are to take a journey, we must accept the call.

In accepting the call, we — and our characters — have formed a goal. An objective. The story question has been established: *Will the heroic character in our story achieve this goal? Will we, as storytellers, succeed in finishing our story?*

As the story progresses, obstacles appear. The character struggles. Sometimes victory seems assured, but disaster looms and victory eludes the heroic character. Finally, we reach a point when all seems lost and victory impossible. This is the climax or black moment of our story, sometimes called the resurrection, in which the character makes a sacrifice to gain a victory.

Each person is the hero of their own story, and travels along the path of their own journey.

STAGES OF THE HERO'S JOURNEY

THE HERO'S JOURNEY has twelve stages which may occur in different order according to the needs of the story. Although not all 12 stages will occur in every story, each stage has meaning to the journey of the soul.

Where Jack M. Bickham's *scene and sequel* and *stimulus and response* illustrate the *building blocks* of story; Joseph Campbell and Christopher Vogler's heroic journey illuminates the *heart and soul* of story.

In the table that follows, I've used terminology from Christopher Vogler's *The Writer's Journey*.

THE HERO'S JOURNEY

1. *Ordinary World:* Most myths and stories take the heroic character out of the ordinary world, into a fictional story world — a special world. To appreciate the contrast, the story must show at least a glimpse of the heroic character's ordinary world.
2. *Call to Adventure:* The hero is asked to undertake a problem, challenge or adventure which will make it necessary to leave

the ordinary world. The story question appears at this point, prompting the reader to speculate on what will happen to the hero.
3. *Refusal of the Call*: Often, the hero has a very understandable fear of the unknown and refuses the Call, trying to remain in the ordinary world. When this happens, another character or event will draw the hero past this decision point of fear.
4. *Meeting with the Mentor*: One of the most common relationships in mythology is that between hero and mentor. The mentor's role is to prepare the hero to face the unknown perils ahead. Mentors often give something to a hero — knowledge or a magic item — but in the end the mentor cannot remain with the hero. The hero must face the unknown alone. Mythology contains many famous mentors. In Greek myth, Mentor was a loyal advisor of Odysseus, King of Ithaca, while Chiron mentored Hercules and Jason. In Welsh literature and Arthurian mythology, Merlin mentored King Arthur. Mentors may occur at any point in a story, but often first appear near the beginning, urging the hero to undertake the adventure.
5. *Crossing the First Threshold:* The hero finally agrees to undertake the challenge, the adventure, or the journey and crosses the threshold to enter the special world for the first time. At this point the story really gets going, and the action begins.
6. *Tests, Allies, Enemies:* After crossing the threshold into the special world, the hero encounters many tests, allies and enemies. These must be dealt with, used or overcome in the journey as the heroic character learns the rules of the story world.
7. *Approach to the Inmost Cave:* The hero approaches a dangerous place where the object of the quest is hidden. By

entering this place, the heroic character crosses the second major threshold. The approach phase continues through all the preparations for entering the Inmost Cave and confronting the danger that lies within.

8. *Ordeal:* The heroic character confronts their greatest fear and hits bottom. We don't know if they can survive. At this point in the story, the hero must symbolically appear to die, approaching death so closely that the reader experiences this near-death. As a result, the following revival from death will give the reader a feeling of elation and victory.
9. *Reward (Seizing the Sword):* The hero survives the ordeal, or slays the dragon, and takes possession of the treasure. This reward may be a magic sword, a holy grail, or knowledge leading to understanding and the ability to deal with hostile forces. At this stage, Shapeshifters may appear. In surviving the ordeal, the hero has gained understanding.
10. *The Road Back:* In a 3-act play, this is the beginning of act three. The hero must deal with the consequences of seizing the reward. In adventure stories, chase scenes may occur with enemies raging in pursuit. In this stage of the journey, the hero realizes they must eventually return to the ordinary world and makes a decision to do so. However, there are still dangers, tests and temptations ahead.
11. *Resurrection:* The hero must be reborn, cleansed in one last ordeal of death and resurrection before returning to the Ordinary World. The hero is transformed by this black moment and is able to return to ordinary life with wisdom and new depth of soul.
12. *Return with the Elixir:* The hero returns from the resurrection with the magic Elixir, having completed the journey of the soul with honor. Heroes who fail to bring back wisdom or some elixir from the resurrection are, like the

WRITING ROMANCE IN THE 21ST CENTURY: PLOTTING AND PLANNING

protagonist in the movie *Groundhog Day,* tragically doomed to repeat the adventure again and again. In some comedies, the ending shows the hero once again beginning on "the same story" – a new adventure with the same challenge repeated. In tragedies, the hero may die, often having finally achieved wisdom.

HERO'S JOURNEY SAMPLE
The Movie "Sabrina" (1995)

THE FOLLOWING ILLUSTRATES the 12 stages of the romance hero's journey using the 1995 version of the movie *Sabrina,* starring Harrison Ford and Julia Ormond. This movie is a coming-of-age story with Sabrina as the heroic character from whose viewpoint the story is told. A web search for "1995 Sabrina streaming" will yield information where you can watch the movie.

- *Ordinary World*: The 1995 romance movie *Sabrina* begins with Sabrina living on the Larrabee estate as a chauffeur's daughter, yearning for David, the younger Larrabee son.
- *Call to Adventure:* Sabrina is being sent to Paris by her father. Will Sabrina ever find herself and give up her unrealistic dream of love with the romantic and irresponsible David?
- *Refusal of the Call:* Hoping that David will stop her from leaving, and that she can have her happy ever after, Sabrina intercepts him as he leaves a party at the Larrabee house. Disillusioned when she realizes that he hardly knows she exists; she decides to carry on with her plans to go to Paris.
- *Meeting with the Mentor:* Sabrina encounters several mentors in this story. Her father is the first mentor, reminding her that she must leave her dreams with childhood, and accept realistic goals for herself. In Paris, she meets a lover-mentor

who shows her how to see the world through a camera, giving her a new reality. Her boss, a sophisticated Parisian woman urges her to go for long walks where she can "meet herself" in Paris. Each mentor contributes to Sabrina's growth into womanhood.

- *Crossing the First Threshold:* In the 1995 version of *Sabrina* (Harrison Ford and Julia Ormond), she flies to Paris and enters the office of the fashion magazine where she's to work. In the earlier 1954 Audrey Hepburn version, she enters a cooking school in Paris. The change of profession reflects the changing roles of women in society during the 20th Century.
- *Tests, Allies, Enemies:* Sabrina is tested by loneliness in Paris. She makes allies – the photographer who becomes her lover, and the sophisticated Parisian woman she works for. With the help of these allies, she fights her battle with loneliness and begins to grow up and assume her own identity.
- *Approach to the Inmost Cave:* Sabrina returns to the Larrabee home in her new, sophisticated persona. Can she remain whole, or will she be consumed by old fantasies?
- *Ordeal:* Sabrina is met by the charming David, and when he falls for her sophisticated charm, the grown-up Sabrina seems lost. She's trapped in the desire for her childish dream and doesn't realize that David loves her outer image, not her inner self. She is in danger of losing her new-found inner strength (dying). When she goes into the cave (the summerhouse) to meet with David, imagining a romantic interlude, David's brother Lionel appears instead.
- *Reward (Seizing the Sword):* Sabrina confronts Lionel in the cave, knowing he plans to get rid of her by paying her off. Lionel has plans for David's future that include both a marriage for David and an associated corporate merger for

Lionel. In the face of Lionel's opposition, Sabrina regains her power and refuses to be paid off. She has recovered the strength of her mature self, and a new wisdom that will help her fight the battles to come.

- *The Road Back:* Sabrina's new relationship with David is opposed by Lionel, who courts Sabrina with a view to separating her from David. Although Sabrina now realizes that David was only a fantasy, she is now falling in love with the shape-changing Lionel.
- *Resurrection:* Sabrina has a final battle scene with Lionel. When he reveals that he was only pretending to love her, she appears to die (death of self and dreams) and then revives, taking her power back and refusing everything from Lionel except a plane ticket back to Paris.
- *Return with the Elixir:* Sabrina returns to Paris, the "real world" where she found herself. We see that she has learned to resist destruction, even when betrayed by the man she loves. But all is not lost, because Lionel has also gone through an ordeal and a transformation. Sabrina has taught him how to love.

SUMMARY AND NOTES: THE HERO'S JOURNEY

"The structure [of the Hero's Journey] should not call attention to itself, nor should it be followed too precisely ... The stages can be deleted, added to, and drastically shuffled without losing power. — Christopher Vogler

Steps in the Hero's Journey

1. Ordinary World
2. Call to Adventure
3. Refusal of the Call
4. Meeting with the Mentor

5. Crossing the First Threshold
6. Tests, Allies and Enemies
7. Approach to the Inmost Cave
8. Ordeal
9. Reward (Seizing the Sword)
10. The Road Back
11. The Resurrection
12. Return with the Elixir

IN ANY STORY, THE HERO is the character whom the reader most identifies with. Whether the hero travels around the world, beyond our galaxy, or through the territory of the mind, it is the hero's emotional journey which hooks the reader, the listener, or the watcher.

Whether the heroic character is male, female, non-binary, human, canine, werewolf or robot, in order to fulfill their destiny, characters must accept the call to adventure. They will encounter allies, enemies, and life-threatening challenges during the adventure.

For the protagonist who fails to accept the call to adventure, who delays too long or fails the ultimate challenge, the story ends in tragedy.

For lovers, the ultimate challenge is that we can love fully only when we allow ourselves to become vulnerable to our beloved. In doing so, we surrender the right to sole determination of our future.

Love always requires a sacrifice.

Resources: Mythic Structure and Archetypes

CHRISTOPHER VOGLER: *The Writer's Journey: Mythic Structure for Writers, 3rd Edition (2007)*. Vogler gives a thorough exploration of the Hero's Journey, based on the work of mythologist Joseph Campbell, author of *The Hero With 1,000 Faces*.

WRITING ROMANCE IN THE 21ST CENTURY: PLOTTING AND PLANNING

JOSEPH CAMPBELL: *The Hero With 1,000 Faces*. Mythologist Joseph Campbell's famous work combines the insights of modern psychology with the author's understanding of comparative mythology.

CAROL S. PEARSON: *Awakening the Heroes Within: Twelve Archetypes to Help Us Find Ourselves and Transform our World* (2015) and *The Hero Within: Six Archetypes We Live By*. Pearson explores how people can live heroically by activating and applying these archetypes in their lives. Highly relevant for authors who wish to grow powerful, evocative characters that come to life on the page.

13: Diversity and Inclusivity

ON AUGUST 28, 1963, Martin Luther King Jr. said the following words:

> *"I have a dream that one day this nation will rise up and live out the true meaning of its creed: "We hold these truths to be self-evident, that all men are created equal."* — Martin Luther King Jr., I Have a Dream speech, 28 August, 1963.

Ten years later Leonard Nimoy, speaking as Commander Spock of the starship Enterprise, said these words:
*"Infinite diversity in infinite combinations...
symbolizing the elements that create truth and beauty."*

ETHNOCENTRISM & CULTURAL RELATIVISM
DURING MY SECOND WEEK at the University of British Columbia (UBC), I sat in on a friend's anthropology course. As I slipped into a seat at the back of the lecture theatre, the professor was explaining the concept of *ethnocentrism*. I'd never heard the word before, but it made me question everything, and it changed my life.

When the lecture ended, I went straight to the registrar's office, took myself out of a course on comparative forms of government, and signed up for Anthropology 100.

WRITING ROMANCE IN THE 21ST CENTURY: PLOTTING AND PLANNING

UBC in 1966 was the perfect place to be taking a course about other peoples, cultures, and human diversity. The campus was teeming with students from a variety of cultures, colors and ethnicities. Eating, talking, and studying, we explored each other's worlds and realities, our minds focused on a universe of time, space, and new ideas.

The 1960s was a decade of expansion, idealism, and hope. It was also a decade of unrest; political tension from the Cold War between the United States and Russia, and civil unrest inside the U.S. with protests against the United States' involvement in the war between North and South Viet Nam, and the military draft.

Canada opened its borders to a flow of young American anti-war protestors crossing the border between 1965 and 1975, and as Giuseppe Valiante says in his article, *U.S. Vietnam war draft dodgers left their mark on Canada* ...

"While it is still unclear how many men and women sought sanctuary in Canada – the country labelled draft dodgers as immigrants, as opposed to refugees – the federal government estimates up to 40,000 made the journey.

"Most stayed after the war, 'making up the largest, best-educated group this country ever received,' says an archived report on the Citizenship and Immigration website."

— Giuseppe Valiante, The Canadian Press April 16, 2015.

Many of the draft dodgers I met during my university days were highly idealistic, and like so many other immigrants to Canada, they enriched our culture, certainly in British Columbia.

The 1960s were a time for dreams, many of which came true. In May of 1961, American president John F. Kennedy made a commitment to put a man on the moon by the end of the decade. Sadly, Kennedy was assassinated in 1963, but his vision come true and a man walked on the moon in 1969. Meanwhile, every week on television, the original series *Star Trek* with its racially diverse cast was showing us strange new worlds of an expanding universe.

The opening narration to the Star Trek series with its message of galaxy-wide inclusivity became famous amongst Star Trek fans. *"Space, the final frontier. These are the voyages of the starship Enterprise. Its five-year mission: to explore strange new worlds, to seek out new life and new civilizations, to boldly go where no man has gone before."* — James T. Kirk, *opening narration to Star Trek: The Original Series.*

Although it didn't occur to me at the time, that 5-year mission reflected an anthropologist's awareness of the concepts of *ethnocentrism* and *cultural relativism.*

Ethnocentrism, a term coined by William Graham Sumner, is the tendency to look at the world primarily from the perspective of your own ethnic culture and the belief that that is in fact the "right" way to look at the world. This leads to making incorrect assumptions about others' behavior based on your own norms, values, and beliefs. For instance, reluctance or aversion to trying another culture's cuisine is ethnocentric. Social scientists strive to treat cultural differences as neither inferior nor superior. That way, they can understand their research topics within the appropriate cultural context and examine their own biases and assumptions at the same time.

This approach is known as "cultural relativism." Cultural relativism is the principle that an individual person's beliefs and activities should be understood by others in terms of that individual's own culture. A key component of cultural relativism is the concept that nobody, not even researchers, comes from a neutral position. The way to deal with our own assumptions is not to pretend that they don't exist but rather to acknowledge them, and then use the awareness that we are not neutral to inform our conclusions. – Social Science LibreTexts https://socialsci.libretexts.org[1]

SEXUAL ROLES & SEXUAL IDENTITY

---

1. https://socialsci.libretexts.org/

WRITING ROMANCE IN THE 21ST CENTURY: PLOTTING AND PLANNING

I SEE A GREAT SIMILARITY between the 1960s and the first two decades of the 21st century. Both are turbulent times heralding change in the realm of sexual roles and sexual identity.

During the 1960s ...

- The birth control pill gave women sexual liberation and many females staked their rights to fulfil their sexual needs just like men.
- Wainwright Churchill III's scientific study *Homosexual Behavior Among Males: A Cross-Cultural and Cross-Species Investigation* presented homosexuality as a fact of life rather than a sin, crime or disease.
- Queen Elizabeth II gave royal assent to the 1967 *Sexual Offences Act,* decriminalizing private homosexual acts in England and Wales.
- Canada's Minister of Justice — Pierre Elliot Trudeau, who later became Prime Minister of Canada — declared that, "There's no place for the state in the bedrooms of the nation" and "What's done in private between two consenting adults doesn't concern the Criminal Code." After 18 months of debate, Trudeau's bill legalizing same-sex sexual activity became law in 1969.
- The Stonewall riots on New York City marked the start of the modern gay rights movement. The first Gay Pride demonstration took place on New York City's Christopher Street.

The first two decades of the 21st century have seen increasing acceptance of LGBTQ+ diversity, same-sex marriage, and equal gender rights.

- In 2001 the Netherlands became the first country to sign a

same-sex marriage bill.
- In 2003 the United States *Lawrence v. Texas* court decision made consenting same-sex relations legal across the USA.
- In 2005 the Canadian parliament legalized same-sex marriage for all of Canada, followed by the Constitutional Court of South Africa later in 2005.
- In 2011 the United Nations Human Rights Council passed its first resolution recognizing LGBT rights, and the United Nations urged all countries which had not done so to enact laws protecting basic LGBT rights.
- By April 5, 2019 twenty-five countries legally recognized same-sex marriage

Sadly, despite continuing progress, as of this writing homosexuality remains punishable by death in 14 jurisdictions including: Afghanistan, Brunei, Iran, Mauritania, Pakistan, Qatar, Saudi Arabia, Sudan, Yemen, the United Emirates, and parts of Nigeria, Somalia, Syria and Iraq.

OPPRESSED AND UNDERREPRESENTED

IN *Ways to Create Authentic Diverse Characters in your Writing,* author Makayla Smith writes ...

"... it seems that our books are still too often plagued by a lack of diverse characters. Straight, White, Christian characters dominate the pages, and while these characters are valid and their stories should be told, they are not the only stories worth telling. Your story may be a work of fiction, but that does not mean it can't reflect real life. And, just because you may not belong to a certain group doesn't mean you can't write characters who do.

WRITING ROMANCE IN THE 21ST CENTURY: PLOTTING AND PLANNING

"The world is full of people of all different ethnicities, sexualities, and religions. Incorporating these aspects of identity into your writing can make the world and the characters you've created come alive."

RESOURCES FOR DIVERSE WRITING

- *Writers for Diversity: Resources for Diverse Characters.* A Facebook community for writers who are interested in creating diverse characters and worlds. Access Writers for Diversity at https://www.facebook.com/WritersforDiversity/

- *Diversity, Political Correctness and The Power of Language* –by Mikki Kendall. Available at http://bit.ly/diverseandpc
- *How to write better LGBT characters* –by Jody Crossman. Available at http://bit.ly/betterlgbt

NaNoWriMo

NANOWRIMO (NATIONAL Novel Writing Month) is a non-profit organization with the following mission statement: *National Novel Writing Month believes in the transformational power of creativity. We provide the structure, community, and encouragement to help people find their voices, achieve creative goals, and build new worlds — on and off the page.*

The following NoNoWriMo blog articles give excellent inclusivity guidance for authors:

- *We Need Diverse Books: Why Diversity Matters for Everyone* –by Marieke Nijkamp. Available at http://bit.ly/writefordiversity
- *We Need Diverse Books: Novels that Get Representation Right*

–by Aisha Saeed. Available at http://bit.ly/repright
- *We Need Diverse Books: A Guide to Spotting and Growing Past Stereotypes* –by Ellen Oh. Available at http://bit.ly/spottingandgrowing
- *We Need Diverse Books: How to Prepare to Write a Diverse Book* –by I. W. Gregorio. Available at http://bit.ly/preparetowrite

Susan Lyons on
EMBRACING DIVERSITY IN THE MODERN LOVE STORY

ON NOVEMBER 6, 2018, the Vancouver Public Library presented a panel titled "Embracing Diversity in the Modern Love Story." The panelists were Michele Fogal (http://michelefogal.com[2]) and Susan Lyons.

Michele's presentation drew on information she had recently presented in a workshop at the Emerald City Writing Conference. You can find her summary here: http://michelefogal.com/including-diversity-writing/. You might also be interested in her Divine Diversity blog: http://michelefogal.com/divine-diversity/

The following is Susan Lyon's presentation.

Introduction

I'D LIKE TO START WITH four quotes. First, from NYT bestselling romance author Suzanne Brockmann in her Romance Writers of America® 2018 Lifetime Achievement Award speech:

"How are readers ever going to expand their worldview if they don't get to meet characters like my adorable gay sheriff?"

---

2. http://michelefogal.com/

WRITING ROMANCE IN THE 21ST CENTURY: PLOTTING AND PLANNING

Next, from Terese Marie Mailhot, a British Columbia author from the Seabird First Nation, in "Heart Berries: A Memoir" (Doubleday Canada; 2018):

"*Indian girls can be forgotten so well they forget themselves.*"

Next, from actor LeVar Burton in an interview with Tom Power on CBC Radio's Q (November 2018):

"*It's hard to underestimate the power [of] seeing yourself reflected in the popular culture ... It validates you. Absent seeing yourself represented or people who are like you represented in popular culture, you are sent a very dangerous message. A message that says you don't matter.*"

And finally, from Ontario hip hop artist Shad – Shadrach Kabango – in "*The Fool Pt 1 (Get it Got it Good)*":

"*Wanna be free?*
Just answer one question, but answer honestly
What are you afraid of?"

Words have power and we must wield that power responsibly. Everyone deserves to have their story told – to read stories that include them and resonate with them rather than marginalize them. And when members of privileged groups read those stories, it helps them understand that we're all just human beings, struggling to live our lives, and there's nothing to fear from people who are different from us.

My Writing Journey

I grew up in a middle-class white community in Victoria. In my high school, of 1,000 students, two were people of colour. Then, when I went to university, a sociology professor opened my eyes to a much broader world, one that wasn't so Leave-it-to-Beaverish, one that had colour and diversity and vibrancy – and prejudice and persecution.

Later, after getting a law degree, I moved to Vancouver, a beautifully diverse community where I could walk down Robson Street and hear a dozen different languages spoken around me. Where my best friend was lesbian and the man I dated was an immigrant from Jamaica.

A while after that, in the 1990s, I started writing fiction.

The first thing I was told was that Canadian settings didn't sell to US publishers and readers. I wasn't told — but it was obvious — that romance novels had white heterosexual heroines and heroes who did not have disabilities. It was almost impossible in Canada to find anything different. As Suzanne Brockmann said earlier this year, while making her Lifetime Achievement Award speech at the Romance Writers of America® conference, the publishing industry is based on "homophobic racist white supremacy."

As an aside, I'll say that things have improved since I started out. But not by leaps and bounds, that's for sure. In 2017, the percentage of romance novels written by people of colour and published by Random House was .01%. For Avon, it was 4.7%. For Harlequin series books, it was 6.6%. Those figures are from *The State of Racial Diversity in Romance Publishing*, a survey conducted by the Ripped Bodice romance bookstore in California.

To get back to my writing journey, at first I tried to write the kind of stories publishers were buying. But it didn't feel right.

It wasn't the world I saw around me in Vancouver, an inclusive one rather than an exclusive one that erased marginalized groups. Nor was it a world I wanted to live in.

Besides, where was it proclaimed that only a white heterosexual woman or man – not just free of disabilities but also exceedingly attractive – deserves to love and be loved?

Knowing that a publisher might never buy my work, I still set my stories in Canada and wrote about the kind of people I knew and wanted to know. And guess what? In 2005, Kensington, a New York publisher, bought my book *Champagne Rules*, set in Vancouver, with a Caucasian heroine and an African-American hero. The publisher had an extremely difficult time finding a stock photo for the cover that featured a couple like that – because there was so little demand – but they did find one. Kensington also bought *Hot in Here*, the second

WRITING ROMANCE IN THE 21ST CENTURY: PLOTTING AND PLANNING

book in that Awesome Foursome series, with a Chinese Canadian heroine and a Caucasian hero. They didn't find a stock photo for that one.

Over the years, I've written:

- heroes who are African American; Indo Canadian; half-Indo Canadian; half-black half-Latino; part Indigenous Canadian; and part Indigenous Australian
- heroines who are Chinese Canadian; Jewish; half-black half-Chinese; part Indigenous Canadian; and in my latest book, *Sail Away with Me,* Japanese Canadian (and yes, there's an Asian woman on the cover)
- recovering alcoholic heroes and heroines
- a heroine who has bipolar disorder; one who is diagnosed with multiple sclerosis; and one who has a son with cerebral palsy
- a hero who's a war veteran amputee with PTSD
- a widowed heroine who survived domestic physical and sexual abuse
- a hero and a heroine (brother and sister) who were raised by a single parent mother who was an addict and a sex worker
- and in *Sail Away with Me,* a hero who survived child sexual abuse

Although the publishing lines I've written for don't include LGBTQ+ romance, or protagonists who are older (and of course the elderly are another marginalized group), there were no objections to having secondary characters from those groups. So, for example, I have a pair of 80-something retired female schoolteachers who, after trying to pass as straight all their lives, reunite after more than half a century and get married.

Does What I do Matter?

After 9-11, a lot of romance writers, like people in many other occupations, asked themselves whether what they were doing had enough value in this scary new world. To me, giving diverse characters a voice, showing positive friendships and romantic relationships, highlighting the ways people face challenges and do the painful work to be stronger, better people, and showing that every decent human being deserves to love and be loved, has been a worthwhile contribution.

Today – midterm election day in the United States – we are very aware of living in a world where there's a lot of stereotyping and fear and hatred and violence aimed at differences – where many people see we/they distinctions rather than seeing each of us as unique individuals who are all in this world together and can only make it a better place if we embrace diversity, if we respect, appreciate, and listen to each other.

As writers, we're often told to "show, not tell." Preaching about the value of inclusion and diversity may alienate some readers, but *showing* diverse characters in fiction and making them relatable is, I think, a way of wielding the power of words responsibly.

Here's some reader feedback:

- First: *"I really admire you for your strong beliefs on the mixing of races. You apparently don't care what color anybody is, whether they are black or white or somewhere in between, and you make a strong case for your view."*
- Second: *"I personally have been diagnosed with bipolar. I think bringing a mental condition into attention and dealing with it as you have is very important in gaining public recognition and acceptance."*
- Third: *"I want there to be books and movies and advertising that represent the world I live in because one of these days, some woman is going to learn that her son loves my Asian daughter, and I want that woman to have already fallen in love with people of color that she's discovered through art and*

WRITING ROMANCE IN THE 21ST CENTURY: PLOTTING AND PLANNING

entertainment. My hope is that she doesn't see an Asian girl, but just a beautiful woman from the inside out – and love her the way I do."

And don't we all hope for that?

What Right do I Have?

What right do I have to write about characters who are people of colour, have disabilities, or are LGBTQ+? Is it cultural appropriation? Am I taking publishing slots that should go to authors who come from those marginalized groups?

Well, no question we should be doing everything we can to encourage these authors, and to encourage publishers to publish them. Look for these kinds of books, read them, tell your friends. Please. A term that's often used now is "*ownvoices*," referring to authors who have the same marginalized identity as their characters.

But on the other hand, if I as an author of romance and women's fiction don't include those kinds of characters in my books, what would I be writing about? Communities consisting solely of white heterosexual able-bodied people? Well, there I'd be, back where I started, creating worlds that don't resemble the real one, and erasing diversity.

My co-panelist Michele Fogal has a wonderful quote on her Divine Diversity website[3] from Saskatchewan author Guy Gavriel Kay:

> "... how the hell could a Y-chromosome carrier ever get a woman right??? ... isn't this what good writing, imaginative empathy, is all about? If not, how could I (or you, or anyone) ever create a geriatric, a psychopath, a grieving widow or widower ... until and unless we were one? If you follow the implications ... far enough, none of us can write anything but autobiographical characters!"

---

3. http://divinediversity.com/index.php/2018/10/30/diversity/

VANESSA GRANT

How do I Write Diverse Characters?

So, when I write multicultural characters, characters who have disabilities, or LGBTQ+ characters – as with all characters who are different from me: men, 20-something women, parents, people who've been widowed or abused or whose marriage is failing, a male bush pilot, a female fire chief, an exotic dancer – I do my best to understand them, to respect them, and to portray them with authenticity.

I do factual research, read fiction, and interview people. I do my best to put myself in my characters' shoes, to draw on things from my own experience to help me identify with others. I am white, middle class, cis, straight, and have no disabilities. But I am a woman and I know how hurt and mad and exhausted and frustrated I feel when I even read about discrimination against women. So, in some ways I can relate to what it's like to be a member of a group that is consistently treated as second-class.

The other thing I do is remember that we are each unique. No two Japanese Canadian women are the same, although if their families – like Iris's in *Sail Away with Me* – lived in British Columbia during World War I and World War II, then prejudice and persecution, internment camps and deportation, are part of their history and will affect them. But because of their unique families and personalities and other life circumstances, those effects will manifest differently in each woman.

As I write, I dig deeper and deeper into each character's backstory and psyche, to truly understand them, to make them as unique and multidimensional as each of us are. And when I'm lucky, they come alive on the page and it feels like they're directing my fingers.

I also have readers review my manuscripts, or parts of them, before submitting them to my editor. "Sensitivity readers" are people who vet a manuscript with sensitivity to a particular issue – as when a woman

WRITING ROMANCE IN THE 21ST CENTURY: PLOTTING AND PLANNING

with MS read the manuscript of *Love Me Tender*. Editors are also becoming increasingly sensitive to issues of diversity and cast a more careful eye than in the past.

Please Read Diversely

If you're interested in reading diversely, here are some places to start:

- CBC Radio interviews and the CBC Books Reading Lists[4]
- Goodreads Listopia
- library catalogues and librarians
- online search engines to find articles and lists, and
- search for hashtag #ownvoices

I promise, it will be worth it!

INTERNATIONAL BESTSELLING author **Susan Lyons** *(who also writes as Susan Fox and Savanna Fox) has written twenty-four novels and eight novellas for Kensington and Penguin Random House. She has also self-published two novels and a dozen collections of short stories. Almost all of her books are set in British Columbia, and they feature multicultural characters and combine romance with serious contemporary issues. They have won numerous awards and have been published in six languages as well as in audiobook format. Visit Susan at susanlyons.ca*

---

[4] https://www.cbc.ca/books/readinglists

14: A Personal Note about Diversity from Vanessa Grant

I AM FORTUNATE TO HAVE the experience of living in a diverse family. Although both my husband Brian and I are descended from a European salad of British, Irish, Scots. German, and Scandinavian; our children and grandchildren have broadened the diversity of our family to include Japanese, Taiwanese, Indigenous First Nations, a member of the LGBTQ community, and by adoption, a gentle Siberian Husky said to be descended from the ancestors of the wolf.

I'm proud of our diversity. Like snowflakes, each person is unique, with their own strengths, flaws, graces, goals, and history. As humans, we weave webs that tie us together and build bridges to expand our experience of humanity.

It is my hope that, like an anthropologist, we strive to treat cultural differences as neither inferior nor superior, to realize that there is no one right way to look at the world; and to acknowledge both our own biases and our assumptions.

As storytellers, we can open our arms, minds, and hearts to the universe of people, heritage, history, and culture ... and enrich the world by *Writing for Diversity*.

We're not perfect. We never will be, but reaching out with an open mind and heart can make the world a better place for all life.

Copyright

Copyright 2019, Vanessa Grant
Cover design by Angela Oltmann
This book contains some revised content previously published by Self Counsel Press under the title *Writing Romance* .

Don't miss out!

Visit the website below and you can sign up to receive emails whenever Vanessa Grant publishes a new book. There's no charge and no obligation.

https://books2read.com/r/B-A-VRB-TJTT

BOOKS 2 READ

Connecting independent readers to independent writers.

Did you love *Writing Romance in the 21st Century: Plotting and Planning*? Then you should read *Lifelines: Kate's Story* by Vanessa Grant!

This book contains mature content.

Kate Taylor hasn't had a good night's sleep since her husband David died. It doesn't help that David's dog, Socrates, watches her constantly as if he expects her to bring his master back; that her personal life is a series of telephone conversations with her evasive adult daughter and her demanding mother; that working as a family counselor she regularly faces a client named Rachel, a narcissistic woman who evokes Kate's most painful memories.

Kate is exhausted: tired of coping, tired of listening, tired of life. Then one night on an icy road, she goes into a treacherous skid. A razor's edge from death, she realizes she wants to live.

She makes plans. She sets goals. She takes a lover. She copes with her daughter's newest crisis and her mother's financial foolishness. Then Kate discovers something about Rachel that throws her into an ethical nightmare.

Her career could be destroyed.

... so could her life.

Read more at vanessagrant.com.

About the Author

Vanessa Grant began her literary career writing the column *A Letter From Lucy Island Lighthouse* for a small northern British Columbia newspaper. She has written over 30 romance novels, been translated into 15 languages, and sold over 10 million copies of her books worldwide.

Vanessa's non-fiction book *Writing Romance* won the Under the Covers literary award and was described in a *National Writer's Monthly* review as "by far the best writing book I have ever read."

Read more at vanessagrant.com.